Disciple Mentoring

Theological Education by Extension

Sam W. Burton

by

Sam Westman Burton

Unless otherwise noted, Scripture taken from the HOLY BIBLE, NEW INTERNATIONAL VERSION. Copyright © 1973, 1978, 1984 International Bible Society. Used by permission of Zondervan Bible Publishers.

Cover art by Dan Battermann.

Published by
William Carey Library
P.O. Box 40129
Pasadena, California 91114
(626) 798-0819

Library of Congress Cataloging-in-Publication Data

Disciple mentoring: theological education by extension / by
Sam Westman Burton.
    p. cm.
  Includes bibliographical references.
  ISBN 0-87808-279-4 (alk. paper)
  1. Seminary extension.
I. Burton, Sam Westman, 1926-
BV4164.B87 1998   97-49878
230'.071'1--dc21   CIP

Printed in the United States of America

TABLE OF CONTENTS

LIST OF FIGURES

FOREWORD

Tragically, and ERRONEOUSLY, many casual observers have mistaken Theological Education by Extension (TEE) for just another form of education, and an inferior one at that. However, the crucial and astounding fact pressing for recognition is that TEE is actually a superior form of leadership discovery, selection, and development.

Take a look. Everywhere around the world the "mainstream" Christian traditions have all skidded to a standstill in their growth while nonstandard forms of the faith have burgeoned. Why? Not because the avalanche of new movements possesses a superior theology but because—more than any other factor—they have found out how to discover and elevate their real leaders.

Yes, there it is: two million leaders in the mission lands have emerged, have surfaced in these "other" movements. The non-standard movements have operated in a way that empowers such leaders without piling up bureaucratic demands.

With only the Bible in hand these real leaders have gained their knowledge in the most powerful learning environment in the world—the local congregation—amidst human problems which a seminary environment is hard pressed to duplicate. Sure, they lack much that the seminary could give them. It is not their fault. The seminaries, for the most part, will not accommodate them.

Unless the "proper" schools can discover the techniques of distance education they will not be able to add anything to the already-rich real-world education in which these two million functional pastors are ministering and thriving. Let's face it: at this time in history it is not "standard Christianity" that is growing.

This book is a very brief, simple explanation of how it is done. It is filled with insight born of actual experience, bristling with practicality and the unassailable reality of true success, even on a small scale. It is impossible for us to set aside this kind of full-blown "Just Do It" example. We must try harder to correctly evaluate the needs of those two million "protoleaders" who seek to follow the Christ we may be underestimating, the Christ who surges in the hearts of real people who are doing the real work of pastoral leadership all across the world.

We need to face the fact that there are more sincere (but "untaught") followers of Christ OUTSIDE the mainstream of Christianity than there are INSIDE. And this is the growing edge. This is the FUTURE!

However, this awesome trend must not continue without needed modification! There is "a more excellent way." The best from both approaches to leadership development can be combined (merging training with gifting) if only we relearn the simple outlines of nonstandard theological education. Such reengineering will take all the resources of the existing seminaries—and more. Yet, it is eminently doable as this little book displays so humbly, and we must do it! Also, it is crucially important as the many questionable deviations of Biblical insight unfold in the rough and tumble of a massive global movement to faith—which is by now clearly out of the Westerner's control.

The school approach we are now promoting is no answer. What good is duplicating such schools in places where the real leaders of grass-roots congregations cannot attend them? That is not the solution. More money poured into more institutions which recruit only untried young people is not the answer.

In the last week I sat with two leaders from different parts of Africa. One talked to me about Nigeria, the largest of the African countries. There are almost two thousand denominations there, now under a new Baptist president. The ECWA movement, even in its standard form encompasses three million souls in perhaps 6,000 congregations of some sort. But, of the 1,800 denominations in Nigeria guess which ones are growing the fastest? (And they are in the vast majority!) The nonstandard ones. Simply, the growing ones harvest their real leadership more effectively, even though they all have access to the power of the Gospel.

My other visitor told of an incident in another country from which he had just returned. He described a sophisticated city congregation with doctors and lawyers and government people in its pews—and an eloquent, quite knowledgeable speaker in the pulpit. Alas, the speaker could not be ordained. Why? He was "a layman." He had not been sanctified by a fixed educational process. This describes the ecclesiastical dead hand upon the church of Jesus Christ all around the world.

Read this book to see how we can find such "protoleaders," enhance them, fully qualify them, and help enable them rather than sideline them. This plan is relatively simple, impressively workable, and spiritually powerful. All it does is show how we can work with God as He "surfaces" key people who may or may not fit into our preconceived educational procrustean bed, and take high-quality education to them by known processes. Ready? This book is for you.

Ralph D. Winter
Frontier Mission Fellowship
Pasadena, California
December 2000

ACKNOWLEDGMENTS

After a missionary career of thirty-eight years, I cannot possibly acknowledge all those who have helped me in my life and ministry. I will, therefore, begin with my experience with TEE. I was a church-planting missionary on the Amazon River in Brazil in 1974. I had tried all kinds of leadership training with varying degrees of success. Then Bill Smallman, director of the Baptist Seminary in Manaus, Brazil, introduced me to TEE.

For four years I discipled through TEE and prepared leaders for the churches. What a blessing! During this time (while on the Amazon), I also studied with the Inservice Program of the School of World Mission (SWM) of Fuller Seminary. These studies on *Church Growth* with Donald McGavran and C. Peter Wagner, and on *Training the Ministry* (TEE) with Ralph Winter and Fred Holland were what helped me with philosophy and insight into TEE methodology.

At the SWM in Pasadena from 1978-1980, Holland continued to encourage me in his course on *Programmed Instruction*. From 1980 to 1994, I was the director of TEE as a member of the Tecate Mission ministering throughout Mexico and into Guatemala. During this time, it was a joy to disciple Carl Olson, Roland Rose and John Forcey for TEE leadership. They continue to carry on this ministry throughout Mexico and Central America.

I want to acknowledge the encouragement received from Gary Coombs, missions chairman of Christian Heritage College and missions pastor of Shadow Mountain Community Church (and now president of Southern California Bible College and Seminary in El Cajon), and the late Otto Reese, president of

Linda Vista Seminary, who have encouraged me to complete a D.Min. which included this dissertation. Ralph Winter, the founder-director of the U.S. Center for World Mission, has also encouraged me with this manuscript. Also, I want to thank James Emery and Wayne C. Weld who have read the manuscript and have given invaluable suggestions on bettering the material.

This document would not have been completed without the fantastic work of Carrie Mann of Christian Heritage College.

I want to acknowledge my lovely wife of almost fifty years, Betsy, mother of our eight children, my companion and missionary helper. May I say to you, Betsy, and to all those mentioned above, "thank you."

Above all, I am grateful and thankful to my wonderful Lord and Savior who saved me and called me into his service of discipling others "to the praise of the glory of his grace" (Ephesians 1:6, KJV).

INTRODUCTION

Throughout the centuries the problems of training others for leadership has not been an easy assignment. Of course, not all leaders have wanted to train others or to "work themselves out of a job" or to train others for co-equal leadership. And then there is the question of how and what materials or methods one should use in training others. In the United States we have been aware of "one-on-one" discipleship or "group discipleship" philosophies and methods. We have used the Navigators, Campus Crusade for Christ, Evangelism Explosion, Inter-Varsity Christian Fellowship, and other ways to complete the Great Commission of making disciples of all nations (Matthew 28:19).

In missionary work throughout the world, missionaries are vitally interested in preaching and teaching the gospel, establishing functioning local churches, and preparing leadership. They do want to work themselves out of a job. We missionaries, naturally, have used training philosophies and systems of theological education which we have learned in traditional institutions in our countries of origin and according to our cultural heritage.

Therefore, we have not only taken the Word of God with its absolutes but also our own cultural baggage with us to the mission field. This includes our structures for theological education.

In this book I would like to present an alternative structure for theological education—Theological Education by Extension (TEE), a movement that has helped in training leaders for the fast growing church throughout the world. Although the computer age and growing philosophies of distance learning are challenging us, Theological Education by Extension continues to be one of the most productive forms for distance education.

We will first consider a biblical perspective on training in ministry as demonstrated in the lives of our Lord Jesus and Paul. We will discuss the search and challenge for alternative forms of adult education, a partial history of TEE, an explanation of the components of TEE, and some of the blessings and problems associated with Theological Education by Extension especially in countries of the two-thirds world. In closing, we include the reports and testimonies of those who are out there doing TEE. The appendices are also important in giving further information or study considerations.

1

A BIBLICAL PERSPECTIVE ON TRAINING IN MINISTRY

Before considering modern day alternative theological education, we should look at a brief biblical perspective on the training of prophets in the Old Testament and the training methods used by Jesus and Paul in the New Testament. These are models for us that are still very valid.

The Old Testament emphasizes the importance and duty of religious teaching and training, but significantly, in the Mosaic economy, does not command the establishment of schools for formal religious instruction.[1]

The home was the first and most effective agency for religious training . . . and the parents were the teachers . . . The training was imparted primarily through conversation, example, and imitation; it utilized effectively the interest aroused by actual life situations.[2]

Actual life situations in the home and in the market place certainly are strong challenges for theological education today.

Later in Israel semi-formal religious instruction from the priests and Levites can be observed. Ineffective teaching by corrupt priests was supplemented by the prophets, the first being Samuel. He instituted a "school of the prophets" at Rammah (I Sam. 19:19-20) and served other places. Not all the

1

students had a predictive gift nor did all prophets attend schools.[3]

Later in the history of Israel, probably during the Babylonian Captivity, the synagogue[4] was created. Here, away from their homeland, the Jews gathered for the reading of the Scriptures and prayer. When they returned from captivity, the synagogue became an important educational agency and spread throughout the known world.

The synagogues also became centers for an elementary school system among the Jews. For "advanced theological education" such as Paul received "at the feet of Gamaliel" (Acts 22:3, KJV), rabbis instructed students in the interpretation and application of the laws.[5]

The New Testament has the supreme example of the Lord Jesus Christ as the model teacher. Ralph R. Covell writes,

Jesus was different from other rabbis in the first century in that he did not establish a formal school for the teaching of his disciples. In common with other rabbis, He had a definite content to impart but He claimed that His teaching was directly from God.[6]

As we read the Gospels, we should observe how Jesus taught, whom he taught, and what he taught. Six considerations in the life of Jesus are helpful in considering alternative forms of theological education. First, Jesus taught by example. One of his great lessons was his example of prayer. Luke tells us, "Jesus was praying in a certain place and when he ceased, one of his disciples said to Him, 'Lord teach us to pray, as John taught his disciples'" (Luke 11:1).[7]

Covell summarizes Alexander R. Hay's comment from his book, *The New Testament Order for Church and Missionary*.

He sought their spiritual development. He taught them how to evangelize, to know and use the scriptures, to have faith in God, to minister in the power of the Spirit. He led them to understand and appropriate the life of prayer in the Spirit, and to be absolutely obedient to the will of God. From Him they learned to exercise unwavering faith, to love God and man and to work together in dedication to God's will. In each of these areas it was His example, more than it was His systematized instruction, which enabled them to know what they ought to be and do.[8]

Second, Jesus taught his disciples in living situations. Jesus' teaching was always relevant because his followers were daily involved in the actual world.

Third, Jesus used sound educational principles in starting where the disciples were and teaching them from the known to the unknown. His parables had great teaching value.

Fourth, Jesus taught according to the needs of the individual in a personalized way. People have general needs but also specific needs.

Fifth, part of the learning process is evaluation. Jesus trained his disciples by assessing them.[9] "If we merely impart content to our students and do not take the time to know them, to understand them, and to live with them to the degree that we are able to evaluate them, we are not fully educating them."[10]

Sixth, Jesus believed in those he trained and, therefore, delegated important work to them.
He had confidence that they would be able to carry out this 'mission impossible.' Nothing will help a student to learn faster or to seek to implement his teaching in a better way than to know that his teacher has confidence in him. [11]

The Apostle Paul considered himself to be a teacher (II Tim. 1:11, I Tim. 2:7, Gal. 1:28) and certainly encouraged others to teach others (II Tim. 2:2).

Covell considers Paul's overall teaching strategy and gives us an excellent summary. He writes that Paul did not teach in only one manner but used a variety of techniques. He certainly taught doctrine but not as an end in itself.

Paul was conscious of his audience. He didn't feel that all Christians were leaders but that leaders should be chosen according to the gifts of the Spirit given each one. He certainly taught obedience to God's Word.[12]

Both Jesus and Paul followed the apprenticeship method of discipleship. This was "on the job" training, putting into practice what is learned, and a very effective way of training leaders for ministry.

---

[1] John B. Graybill, "School," in *The Zondervan Pictorial Bible Dictionary*, Merrill C. Tenny, ed. 759.
[2] Ibid, 759.
[3] Ibid, 759.
[4] See article in Appendix on *Synagogue: Form for the Mission of the People of God Among Nations*.
[5] Graybill, 760.
[6] Ralph R. Covell and C. Wagner, *An Extension Seminary Primer*, 34.
[7] Ibid, 35.
[8] Ibid, 36.
[9] Ibid, 37-39.
[10] Ibid, 39.
[11] Ibid, 40.
[12] Ibid, 50.

2

ALTERNATIVE FORMS OF THEOLOGICAL EDUCATION TODAY

Theological education includes all of the biblical and doctrinal teaching of the church of Jesus Christ. The teaching is both theoretical and practical and usually has as its purpose the preparation of leaders for the church.

The traditional system of theological education began in the United States around 1800, and this pattern has been accepted as the norm. What is that pattern? Kenneth Mulholland answers that question.

Generally speaking, that pattern consisted of extracting young, unproven, single, usually male volunteers from their home environment to train them in a centrally located institution, where they resided for about three years. There they were taught the classic theological subjects, mostly by rote, by predominantly missionary professors and a sprinkling of part-time nationals. Academic training was supplemented by practical work assignments in local churches with various degrees of supervision. After three years these young people were declared pastoral material if they had successfully passed the required exams, had expounded no heresy, and had not strayed beyond the bounds of morally acceptable behavior as defined by the sponsoring institution and/or denomination.[1]

James H. Emery agrees that the traditional seminary is

The system of ministerial preparation that was developed in the United States at the beginning of the last century to provide training within the denomination. . . .The system involves resident students who are single and young (with some special arrangements for married people). The classes are arranged according to a schedule that occupies the morning hours especially, when professors who are specialists in their fields have the lectures. There is limited discussion, the students have assigned reading and papers to prepare and can only spend a very limited time working to support themselves. A high level of academic preparation is required for entering in order to have a broad general background, but no experience is required.[2]

Until today, this pattern of theological education has well served the needs of the churches in the United States. However, there is an attitude of professionalism among the clergy that contributes to the growing dichotomy between the clergy and the laity. This was not always the system in the United States. The early colonists used an apprenticeship system which was patterned after the ministries of the Lord Jesus and the Apostle Paul. Ralph Winter describes this concept in his article "An Extension Seminary Manual."

Close examination shows that the Colonial colleges were more like elementary or junior-high-level boarding schools and that specific training for the ministry took place after the period of full time training in 'college,' in a kind of apprenticeship: graduates went to live in a minister's home.[3]

In most rural communities, where ministers worked other jobs such as farming, there was also in-service training used by the Methodists where formal education was minimal but spiritual fervor was considered essential for a call from God. These Methodist circuit riders "served while they studied and studied while they served."[4] This meant they were training in the work rather than for the work. The Baptists were not in a position to use the apprenticeship pattern of the Puritans nor the in-service training followed by the Methodists. The pastors were selected from among them and many had to carry on a tentmaking work while they ministered. They usually had a self-study program for increasing knowledge of theology.[5] The Plymouth Brethren followed this tent-making system as they all over traveled the world to meet the needs of an expanding frontier.

In this brief summary of traditional theological education and patterns of ministry in the United States we have seen some great contrasts. The problems of traditional theological education are apparent in the expanding and growing churches of the two-thirds world. Mulholland expresses the problem in the following manner.

> The tendency of North American theological educators is to seek to impose those models of theological education which are most current in North Atlantic countries upon developing nations rather than explore models which were viable in those same countries when they historically faced some of the same problems which the third world nations now confront.[6]

Wayne C. Weld writes about the *Crisis in Theological Education* and the problems of traditional theological education. He mentions that the established patterns used by mission agencies are often culturally irrelevant, and speaks of areas of inadequacy in the traditional forms. These include the following: the inability to supply rapidly growing churches with pastors; the inordinate expense of pastoral training (which is high even in Third World countries and includes tuition and fees, professors' salaries, building, room and board, etc.); the cultural dislocation of students where often they are unwilling to return or are unable to fit in with their people any longer; the improper selection of candidates for training because of lack of spiritual gifts for ministry or a lack of demonstrated pastoral gifting and experience.[7] On this last point he elucidates,

The criteria for choosing pastoral candidates needs to be carefully reexamined. Young men may be chosen because they are tall, good looking, have a good speaking voice, demonstrate an ability to express themselves well, got good grades in school or possess other such arbitrary qualities.[8]

These do not measure up to the biblical standards for leadership. Most of the spiritual gifts are mentioned in Romans 12, I Corinthians 12-14, and Ephesians 4, while the "job description" for pastoral leaders is found in I Timothy 3 and Titus 1. These qualities are vital for respected leadership in growing and expanding churches.

We have briefly discussed the biblical example of Jesus and the Apostle Paul in their use of an apprenticeship and in-service training system for leaders in the Christian church. We have noticed their example.

Also, we have considered some aspects of the traditional seminary system of theological education and some of the problems involved as the church of Jesus Christ grows throughout the world.

We now will consider some alternative educational forms including a consideration of formal, nonformal, and informal education. We will define these forms and note their advantages and disadvantages as well as some applications to actual life situation.

Edgar J. Elliston explains the meaning of these terms:

Formal education refers to schooling; nonformal education refers to planned learning outside of a schooling environment for which academic credit is not given; informal education refers to the unplanned acculturation/enculturation processes that occur through relationships. Nonformal education is planned out of school learning. The weakness of each type of education is compensated by the strengths of the other two types.[9]

Ted Ward mentions some of the criticisms leveled at formal education.

Ivan Illich charged that schools were a major cause and perpetrator of social inequality (1971). The needs of the poor, the illiterate and the unemployed were ignored. The work of Paulo Freire is associated with attempts to change these situations through nonformal education (1971). The Silberman's Carnegie Commission report notes many other problems such as 1) the emphasis on competition; 2) the misuse of educational resources; 3) the misuse of time due to an obsession with sequential curriculum grades, tests, registers and administrative details; 4) the general use of coercion, manipulation, and discipline to fit individual students into a pattern that will reflect the teacher's not the student's attitudes toward life, education and learning; 5) the neglect of social-emotional growth; 6) the absurdity of the teacher-versus-student relationship; 7) the loss of real, relevant, meaningful and rewarding, experiences in school; and 8) the belief that the classroom and school is the only learning environment available to students and teachers.[10]

What are some examples of nonformal education? Examples include literacy classes, boy and girl scouts, organized sports, and occupational training for many vocations.

Elliston cites Simkins who describes the contrasts between the three kinds of education.

Formal and nonformal education are separated from informal education through being purposely organized and directed to facilitate particular kinds of learning. Informal education is not organized with the achievement of specific learning objectives in view, but rather is educational in a more general and implicit way.[11]

Nonformal and formal education are also contrasted by relating to three major problems in formal education: cost, relevance to students, and flexibility.[12] Elliston helps us understand these three modes of education.[13]

Formal Education
School based, planned learning
Certificate/diploma/degree oriented
Theoretical
Future oriented
Strong in content

Nonformal Education
Planned out of school learning
Function oriented rather than certificate oriented
Practical
Present oriented

Informal Education
Unplanned learning
Practical
Immediate orientation (generally)
Personal, individualized, relationship based
    development
Strongly affects values and attitudes

For further explanation of these concepts, see Elliston's *Developing Leaders at a Distance: Contextualizing Leadership Development.* These concepts will help us understand the "why" of the "birth" of Theological Education by Extension.

---

[1] Mulholland, 3-4.
[2] Emery.
[3] Winter.
[4] Mulholland, 8.
[5] Ibid, 9.
[6] Ibid, 10.
[7] Weld, *World Directory* 7-14.

---

[8] Ibid, 14.
[9] Elliston, *Developing Leaders at a Distance* 13-14.
[10] Ward, *Handbook of the Nonformal Education Institute.*
[11] Elliston, *Theological Education by Extension* 102.
[12] Ibid, 103.
[13] Ibid, 101.

3

A PARTIAL HISTORY OF THEOLOGICAL EDUCATION BY EXTENSION

Having considered alternative forms of education, we can now turn to the historical happenings in Guatemala which brought on the movement called Theological Education by Extension (TEE).

When my wife and I were on the Amazon River in Brazil, we learned that there were some 16,000 evangelical pastors shepherding the rapidly growing church in Brazil. Only 4,500 of these had any theological training and there was a great need for some way of training these leaders who were already in the ministry. In 1974, we had been in Brazil for nine years (after serving in Uruguay and Argentina for seven years), when we heard about TEE and began training our own leaders on the Amazon. But, when and how did this nonformal movement begin?

It was spoken of as *The Emergence of a Movement*[1], *The Birth of the Extension Seminary*[2], and *A Modest Experiment Becomes a Model for Change*[3].

But how and why did it all begin? James Emery who was there at the time writes,

Most ideas do not spring full blown into the mind, neither did TEE. . . . From the beginning of my time in Guatemala

13

in 1953 some problems were evident. During my first days I was taken to two presbytery meetings to which I became an associate member. One part of the meetings included a time for the examination of ministerial candidates on their courses of study. . . . During my first furlough I studied in the agricultural college at Cornell University, where the New York State Cooperative Agricultural Extension work centered, and many courses focused on how to make the programs effective. The agricultural extension work taught using non-formal and adult education methods and were effective in raising the standard of agricultural work in the state. The first month of this furlough Ralph Winter was with me, appointed to go to Guatemala. We had known each other since 1946 when we were in seminary together. We discussed many of the issues related to the work in Guatemala. Later I studied the courses related to agricultural extension work. The name "Theological Education by Extension" came from this association with these agricultural extension programs. . . . Ralph Winter arrived on the field in 1958 after language school, and we spent many long hours discussing all the issues of training, for pastors, workers, and ordinary believers who need not only an understanding of the Bible and the Gospel, but also a way to make a decent living.

The program of TEE began in 1962 after a number of experiments beginning in 1955. It expanded in 1962 to over 200 students.

Nineteen sixty-four was a significant year for TEE. There had been a chance meeting in 1963 (At a WCC meeting in Mexico) between Ralph Winter and Dr. Jim Hopewell of the Theological Education Fund (TEF). Dr. Hopewell had heard of the experiment in Guatemala, and following this encounter arranged to visit the Seminary. After this visit we requested and received funds from the TEF to upgrade the library, to provide some scholarship money for two members of the faculty, and to provide for a trip to study

Programmed Instruction. . . . . One of the major problems of TEE, as all have recognized, relates to the materials for study. . . . One request was for funds for me to visit the USA during the school vacation and learn about Programmed Instruction. We came to the USA and I visited a number of places where people were working with PI, Moody Bible Institute, Rochester-Colgate Seminary, the Presbyterian Board of Christian Education, and especially Teachers College, Columbia University. I obtained many books, discussed the issues with a number of people involved and read rather widely. . . . Later in some of the presentations Ralph Winter made, and in articles written about TEE, programmed instruction was linked with it. Dr. Ted Ward of Michigan State University, who had been involved in educational technology for some time and had expertise in PI continued the linkage.[4]

Wayne C. Weld also summarizes the circumstances which brought this about.

A form of on the job training had been used by the Presbyterians in Guatemala for more than a quarter of a century. National workers were assigned books to study. Every six months they were tested on their mastery of the materials studied and then were assigned further work. On completion of the entire study program in twelve to fifteen years the men were ordained, recognized as full pastors, and began to supervise the studies of the younger men (Peters 1940: 370). Ordained men could continue their studies toward a degree through correspondence courses. Short term institutes were also held to encourage men in their studies (Peters 1940: 372). This system of in-service training through individual study was still used in the rural presbyteries when Emery and Winter appeared on the scene and may have helped some of the Church leaders accept the idea of a decentralized school. However, the accepted pattern of preparation for the more respected urban ministry was determined by the residence seminary established in the capital in 1938. All of the problems of traditional theological education which were discussed earlier in this study could be found in the Presbyterian Seminary. Not enough pastors were being produced for the growing church. Most of the congregations could not achieve the status of a recognized church because they did not have an ordained pastor. Meanwhile student enrollment in the residence school varied between six and twenty. The needs of the church were not being met.[5]

TEE was the creation of James Emery, Ralph Winter, Jose Carrera B., and Charles Ainley. Winter and Emery had much in common, with a background in engineering, seminary, anthropology and other common experiences, which influenced the approach to ministerial preparation. Ross Kinsler arrived in September 1964, at the end of the school year, and began in January 1965 to take an active part in the Presbyterian Seminary.

These missionaries considered the problem of many churches without pastors and were thoroughly familiar with several solutions others had tried in training those who could not enter traditional seminaries: correspondence courses, night schools, regional training institutes, and other methods. But none of these fit their particular set of problems.[6]

By 1958, the Presbyterian Synod had realized that changes had to be made in the seminary. One of the difficulties had been that the seminary was in Guatemala City and was inaccessible to the majority of church leaders. In that year the seminary board made the decision to relocate in the western part of the country, central to three presbyteries and most of the churches. After much debate the seminary was moved in 1959 to San Felipe, Reu. Changes in the rural areas at this time made it impossible for laymen to take time off from sharecropping as was previously done. Instead of being able to attend month-long study periods, they had become employees and could only study evenings and weekends. Thus began the idea of the decentralized seminary. If the leaders could not come to the seminary, then they would take the seminary to the leaders.[7]

Regional centers were set up where the students came once a week to meet with the professor from the seminary. The students would have to take home assignments and use the same textbooks as the resident school. This seemed to work, and the enrollment increased almost immediately from seven to fifty students. But it became evident that this inductive type of study was too difficult for many of the students.

The missionaries focused on the problem and its solution and saw the value of self-instructional study materials, something that had already been widely accepted by educational psychologists. The missionaries would write new textbooks to fit the educational levels and cultural relevance of their leaders. This was not an easy task and demanded much creativity and discipline.[8]

There were flaws in the program that have been worked on since 1962, but the advantages far outweighed the shortcomings. Ralph Winter has listed five of the advantages.

1. The door was opened for leaders who desired to reach a higher level of training.
2. The leaders could receive their theological training within the context of their own subculture.
3. The system permitted those students who had low motivation to leave without losing face.
4. Instead of lowering academic levels, it was observed that the extension student learned better and developed better study habits in his/her home.

5. The project was more economical than the conventional seminary and it saved much time for the professor.[9]

But, where did the movement go from these humble beginnings? Kenneth Mulholland tells us.

In 1966, theological education by extension (TEE) was limited to a single seminary in one nation. Eight years later the movement encompassed 16,475 [students] in 182 institutions in 57 countries. Born and nurtured in growing Third World churches, it is now being tried successfully in the United States as well as those in the Third World institutions long dominated by traditional North American and European patterns of theological education. TEE has struck ministerial training with such force that some enthusiasts label this as the most important innovation in theological education in this century. Not only has it responded directly to the felt needs of churches around the world but has had a widespread indirect influence.[10]

Wayne Weld also expounds on this point that:

Many institutions and theological educators do not participate directly in extension programs have, nevertheless, reflected the influence of the movement as they modify their philosophy and methods of teaching. The widespread acceptance of extension studies has also encouraged others to promote other forms of ministerial and lay training which are even less traditional or 'nonformal.' The whole concept of the ministry has been called into question and is being examined anew from perspectives which are at the same time more pragmatic and more biblical.[11]

From Guatemala the vision and movement spread to Ecuador, Honduras, the West Indies, Mexico, Costa Rica, a workshop-consultation held in Armenia, Colombia, in September, 1967, and then on to Brazil and Bolivia, Asia, Africa, Indonesia, and many other parts of the world.

F. Ross Kinsler edited the book *Ministry by the People, Theological Education by Extension*. The book illustrates the extension movement in all parts of the world and is very helpful in illustrating the value of extension studies. We will consider some of the articles:

LATIN AMERICA AND THE CARIBBEAN
1. "Study by Extension for All Nations—Passing on the Faith," by Michael Crowley.
   The name SEAN is taken from the third person plural of the Spanish verb "to be" found in 2 Timothy 2:2, where the instruction is given to Timothy to hand on the apostle's teaching to faithful people who will in turn be able to teach others. The choosing of this name and text by the initial group of extension writers highlighted their intention of doing something about the teaching and mobilizing of Christians in the local churches of the southern cone of South America. The project was born in 1971 when the then Anglican bishop of northern Argentina asked missionary Anthony Barrett to set up an extension program to teach the churches. Conveniently, the word SEAN also served as a title of the Anglican extension program (Seminario por Extension Anglicano). The interdenominational and international character of the program soon brought about a third meaning for the name: Study by Extension from All Nations![12]
   SEAN was born of the necessity for trained Church leaders in 1971. The number of Protestant pastors in Latin America was at about 100,000 with only 20% having theological training. The some 400 Latin American Bible institutes could not meet the challenge or fulfill the need of the growing church. SEAN grew with limited financial resources and much missionary endeavor but produced programs that have been adopted for use throughout Latin America. They have written good texts that have been field tested. One of their

most popular series is used with much profit throughout Latin America.[13] It is a six-book compendium based on Matthew's Gospel and purposes to teach each student the following principles:

—a thorough knowledge of the life and ministry of Christ in its historical, social, and political setting;

—an analysis of the Gospel of St. Matthew and its relationship with the other Gospels;

—a grounding in the fundamentals of the Old Testament and how it relates to the coming of Christ and his ministry;

—the techniques of simple Bible text analysis, so students can tackle the Scriptures in personal study;

—an outline of systematic theology;

—an appreciation of the teachings of mainstream Christianity and the teachings of sects that the students are likely to encounter;

—techniques of study, thinking and application (often not learnt in previous education);

—practical and pastoral theology with special emphasis on the ministry in the local church—Bible Study (personal and private), worship and liturgy, preparation of simple sermons/messages, evangelism (personal and team).[14]

In 1980, SEAN set up an extension program for Anglican churches in the Valparaiso-Vina del Mar areas of Chile. There has been great enthusiasm and success here and among many denominations throughout Latin America as they use "the Matthew course." We can testify of its blessing as we work and travel through Mexico and Guatemala and work with Hispanic churches in California. The "Matthew course" from SEAN is alive and well in 2001! The "Abundant Life" course of eighteen lessons is also widely used. SEAN continues to team write materials for higher levels of study.[15]

2. "Theological Education and Evangelism by Extension" by George Patterson.

George Patterson, serving with Conservative Baptist Home Mission Society, developed a vital program of extension in Northern Honduras. No theological textbooks existed at the level of the people with whom he was working. He noticed that the people were reading something! Photonovels! He wrote his own materials at the level of the people, materials that allowed each person to proceed at his/her own pace. He related education to the local church, presented obedience-oriented education, and established churches through extension chains. The result: seventy-five churches in twenty years! The curriculum was centered around seven basic commands of Christ: repent and believe, be baptized, love, celebrate the Lord's supper, pray daily, give sacrificially, and make disciples.[16] He wrote:

> But don't do it unless you are willing to make a great sacrifice. Making obedient disciples is dangerous for everyone involved. It means asking God for the cross God wants us to bear. It means avoiding traditions and provoking opposition from the traditionalists. Your students will rebel when they see that you want them to be disciples with a military mentality (2 Timothy 2:2-4). But the rewards are worth it, if what Christ said about the kingdom of heaven is true.[17]

3. "Distance Education in a Revolutionary Situation" by Irene Westling Foulkes and Ruben Lores.

The experience of poverty, dependence and exploitation in Latin America imposes on theological institutions a new agenda and a new way of doing theology which takes as its point of departure that kind of experience and the struggles it generates. This starting point, radically different from that of most theologians in North America and Europe, necessarily leads to a rejection of theological orientation and emphases that perpetuate oppression.[18]

Because of this contradiction, the Latin American Biblical Seminary (LABS) of San Jose, Costa Rica, launched in 1976 its Diversified Program at a Distance (PRODIADIS). The idea of distance means that neither students nor professors have to travel long distances from their home base. PRODIADIS is a diversified program and includes nonformal education and life experiences of educational value. The individualized course material offers an open curriculum at a postsecondary level. The program only enrolls students who can meet the educational requirements for university level. The following quote expresses the philosophy:

> Live dialogue, group experience, good libraries, and thorough-going evaluation are all essential for a worthwhile theological education. In stressing the aspects, however, traditional theological education has too often forgotten one over-riding criterion of effective vital involvement with the environment for which the education is supposed to prepare the student to minister.[19]

AFRICA

"Programming for Ministry Through Theological Education by Extension" by Fred Holland.

Holland points out that paternalism continued to be a problem in Africa. There had been financial dependency, theological fears, and a show of forms that were rigid, creations of the West. The theological schools were stagnant. But then an "awakening" came about through concern for contextualization by TEE and in the Association of Evangelical Bible Institutes and Colleges in Africa and Madagascar (AEBICAM) with its concern for relevance and ministry performance.

The TEE model came from the Presbyterian Seminary in Guatemala, and received help from CAMEO workshops and the "rail-fence" introduced by Ted Ward. Later Holland changed the model to a four-part railing model which includes the three parts of the fence but adds the dimension of spiritual formation. As in other areas of the world, there were leadership problems.[20] "Not only did we lack local group leaders, but church leaders on all levels lacked full training to perform their assignments adequately."[21]

There were no suitable TEE books for Africa. Those from other nations were, of course, in a different language and were not culturally relevant. It was necessary for them to produce the missing study books aimed at the thousands of local leaders. They would write a complete Bible school curriculum of programmed textbooks. Holland and his wife worked hard in preparing, writing, programming, and evaluating their texts. Programmed Instruction (PI) seminars were conducted in Zimbabwe, Nigeria, Kenya and South Africa. At one time there were ninety-seven writers who (as writing teams) published twenty-six texts with ten others still in preparation.

Other efforts in Africa are described in "African Independent Churches Adopt Theological Education by Extension" by Peter M. Makamba in Fambidzano (Zimbabwe) and "Training Village Ministries in Tanzania" by Bumija Mshana and others.[22]

ASIA AND AUSTRALIA
"An Indian Approach to Training for Ministry" by Vinay Samuel and Chris Sugden.

The authors explain the necessity for developing forms of theological education that meet the needs of India's growing church.

The Indian context is twenty percent urban and eighty percent rural. Sixty percent of the people live below the poverty line due to religiously sanctioned injustice and exploitation. The Indian church has emerged largely among poor people, and in rural areas it is still mainly composed of the poor. In the urban setting it is increasingly a middle-class church with a growing number of competent middle-class professional people. These people, along with able leaders in rural areas, have a deep commitment to being involved in Christian ministry, but they have no opportunity to become suitably equipped. To help the churches meet this need for training leadership, TAFTEE was formed.[23]

We notice that the Association for Theological Education by Extension (TAFTEE) was formed in 1971 to meet these needs.

TAFTEE's programs developed out of its underlying understanding of mission and ministry. Its understanding is that the whole church must be equipped for mission to address the whole gospel to the whole of life. The whole church must be equipped; all its members must be enabled to develop and use their gifts for ministry.[24]

The authors sum up the program by an evaluation. They write:

Throughout its ten years of existence TAFTEE has been seeking to learn from its context and experience. The first courses included a number of international TEE texts. Now 85 percent of the courses have been written by people living and working in India. Ten percent have so far been written by Indian staff writers. There is a great shortage of theological literature relevant to Christian life and ministry in the Indian context. TAFTEE courses are providing an important source of relevant material. Students particularly value the opportunity to discuss issues of integrity, corruption, strikes, trade unions and family life which are rarely discussed in Christian meetings. The courses provide a library of material that students draw on long after their courses are completed.[25]

In the Philippines, Jose Gamboa, Jr., of the Union Seminary writes of "Alternative Education for Church Workers in the Philippines."[26] And at the Nanking Union Theological Seminary, "Theological Education in New China"[27] was written. For a more complete view of many other countries and programs I would suggest the reading of Kinsler's book. He also edits writings about extension programs in North America and in Europe. It is very worthwhile reading.

And, thus, we notice a movement that had small beginnings but has extended to all parts of the Earth. But after all, what is Theological Education by Extension?

---

[1] Weld, 28.
[2] Covell, 70.
[3] Kinsler, *Ministry by the People*. 33.
[4] This quote is from a forthcoming article to be published entitled *Theological Education by Extension: Origin and Development*.
[5] Weld, 28-29.
[6] Emery, notes, 72-73.
[7] Covell, 72-73.
[8] Ibid, 72-73.
[9] Ibid, 75.
[10] Mulholland, 77.
[11] Ibid, 77.
[12] Kinsler, 42-43.
[13] Ibid, 42-43.
[14] Ibid, 44.
[15] Ibid, 44-50.
[16] Ibid, 52-60.
[17] Ibid, 52-60.
[18] Ibid, 68.
[19] Ibid, 69-72.
[20] Ibid, 103-106.
[21] Ibid, 103-106.
[22] Ibid, 107-115.
[23] Ibid, 239.
[24] Ibid, 241-242.
[25] Ibid, 245.
[26] Ibid, 256-263.
[27] Ibid, 264-273.

4

WHAT IS THEOLOGICAL EDUCATION BY EXTENSION?

We have considered how Theological Education by Extension began in 1963 as an innovative training program for "extending" theological education from a central seminary to where the untrained church leaders were. It was introduced by three missionary trainers: Ralph Winter, Ross Kinsler, and James Emery. Some of the ideas and definitions are given below.

Theological Education by Extension (TEE) refers to a decentralized training program in which equivalent theological training is extended out from centralized resources to decentralized centers where students can remain in an in-service status in their normal community environment.[1]

It is a movement that can and should challenge the church at large, ecclesiastical leaders, theological educators, and the whole people of God—to a new understanding of and participation in ministry and mission. It is useful to look at theological education by extension as a movement and a vision rather than a specific technique or system.[2]

What is extension education? Briefly, it is that method which reaches the student in his own environment rather than pulling him out into a special controlled environment. It isn't necessarily the best method of education for all purposes; it is different. It is a method of education which does not disrupt the learner's productive relation to society. Theological Education by Extension breaks down the dichotomy between clergy and laity by encouraging all kinds of leaders to prepare themselves for ministry. It stimulates the dynamics of ministry at the local level by training those men and women in the context of their own communities and congregations. It enables the congregations to develop their own leadership for ministry so that they do not need to depend on outside, highly trained, professional clergy. (Guatemala Center for Studies in Theological Education and Ministry, Occasional Paper No. 8, San Felipe, Reu, Guatemala).[3]

Ralph Winter makes an interesting point.

TEE can reach out to any man in any local congregation and screen him, prepare him, and elevate him to whatever level any church desires for whatever leadership position his God-given gifts will take him.[4]

Therefore, whatever the specific reasons for each extension program, the shared vision has been to encourage and enable local leaders to develop their gifts and ministries without leaving their homes, jobs, communities, and local congregations.

In summary, the student stays in his/her productive place in society, living with his/her family, and in his/her environment and culture but continues his/her studies with extension courses.

The philosophical and theological basis of TEE counteracts the false dichotomy between clergy and laity in almost all ecclesiastical traditions. It endeavors to be both biblical and educational in training all members of the body of Christ.

TEE is, therefore, in contrast with some other forms of adult continuing education. In the resident school the student studies full time and lives at or near the institution; the curriculum is fixed, the student studies for future productivity, and there is adequate contact between student and teacher. In the correspondence school students of any age or stage study courses from institutions and send them through the mail; there is no immediate "feedback" and the student doesn't meet his/her teacher. Seminar studies are usually short periods of intensive study on weekends or week-long seminars such as summer camps; the purpose is maximum learning in a minimum time slot. Open education permits the student to study whatever course, at whatever hour, in whatever locality, at his/her own pace, with an open curriculum.

Sound biblical bases exist for Theological Education by Extension. Beginning with God's redemptive purpose in Genesis 3:15 and especially through the call of Abraham, we see God expressing his desire to bless the whole world. In the Great Commission there are three participles (going, baptizing, and teaching) and one imperative (make disciples) (Matthew 28:19-20). The whole movement of TEE supports evangelism and church growth. Paul best expresses the purpose of discipling in ministry when he writes to the Ephesians and to Timothy.

> But to each one of us grace has been given as Christ apportioned it. It was He who gave some to be apostles, some to be prophets, some to be evangelists, and some to be pastors and teachers, to prepare God's people for works of service, so that the body of Christ may be built up until we all reach unity in the faith and in the knowledge of the Son of God and become mature attaining to the whole measure of the fullness of Christ. Then we will no longer be infants, tossed back and forth by the waves, and blown here and there by every wind of teaching and by the cunning and craftiness of men in their deceitful scheming. Instead, speaking the truth in love, we will grow into Him who is the head, that is, Christ. From Him the whole body, joined and held together by every supporting ligament,

grows and builds itself up in love, as each part does its work. (Ephesians 4:7, 11-16 NIV)

And the things you have heard me say in the presence of many witnesses entrust to reliable men who will also be qualified to teach others. (II Timothy 2:2 NIV)

Vergil Gerber comments, "Discipling disciplers is the ultimate goal of all Theological Education."[5]

Throughout the brief history of the extension movement there has been a common, over-riding purpose: to extend the resources of theological education to the functioning and developing leaders of the congregations.[6]

The Ephesian concept is illustrated in the chart on the following page which shows the contrast between contemporary and traditional theological practice and extension philosophy.

Figure 1

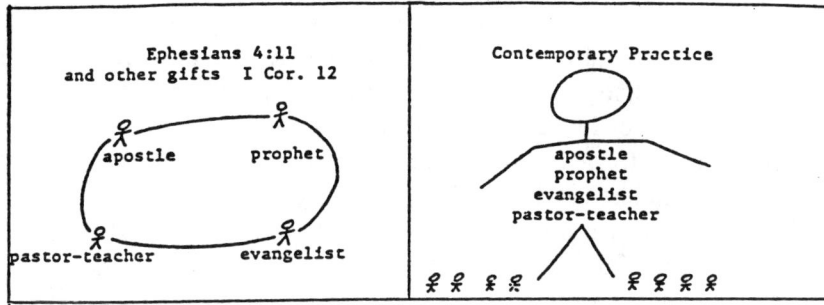

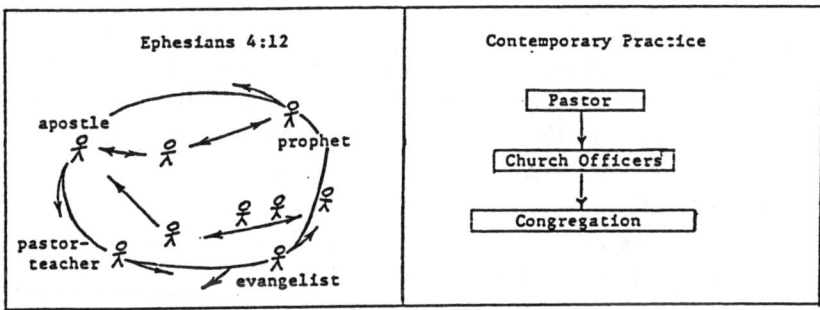

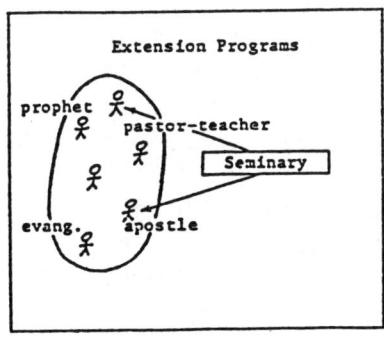
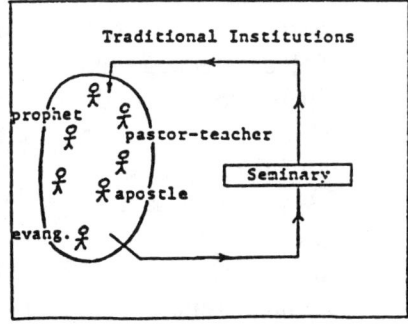

Edgar Elliston helps us understand the characteristics of TEE.

1. The training is made available to functioning leaders with a minimum of extraction from locale and in-service ministry context; that is, the people being trained do not leave their homes and community.
2. Motivation for learning is high since these students are already leaders (at the level of small group or above). This in-service ministry context not only provides motivation for cognitive learning but also stimulates experiential learning.
3. Teachers travel to dispersed extension centers convenient to both teacher and student schedules (usually about once per week). Naturally this delivery system limits the number of courses offered at a center so that a total program of study will probably take three to four times as long as the equivalent centralized program (i.e. a three-year residence program may take ten years to complete).
4. The training in terms of total study time (structured hours) may be equivalent to that which would be offered at the central center since the student spends many more hours in self-study—even through contact hours in the classroom setting is less.
5. In order for the student to spend many more hours in self-study the cognitive input for the course must be packaged in self-study delivery systems that can be used by the student on location without direct access to an instructor.
6. Since actual contact time between student and teacher is less than that of a centralized setting because the student has interacted with efficient self-study materials time spent together is not spent in presenting the cognitive input but is spent in providing the dynamic interaction needed to correlate the cognitive learning with experiential and affective

learning. Thus teachers must operate andragogically as facilitators rather than pedagogically as lecturers.[7]

Theological Education by Extension, of course, is an educational program. There are some very important modern educational principles that help in understanding the vision, the movement of TEE. Elliston considers these educational trends in his syllabus. He cites the important work of Malcolm Knowles in his book, *The Modern Practice of Adult Education—From Pedagogy to Andragogy.*

He . . . showed that in the mid 1930s there was a significant change in the reality of the premises underlying educational philosophy. Until that time the cycles of major social changes took longer to happen than the average life-span of an individual. But due to two factors—the lengthening of life-span due to medical technological advances and the rapidly accelerating pace of change in society—the average person will live through several major society changes. The implications of this for education were slow to be perceived but are being seen more and more in our day. The major implication is this—previous to 1930 a person could be educated with a grasp of all that was needed to be known to live out a lifetime. Since that time knowledge is changing so rapidly and society so rapidly that a person must be retaught several times in order to keep up with the rapid changing society. That is, people can not be educated once and for all. Education is an on-going process.[8]

Malcolm Knowles, the expert in adult education, introduced the term *andragogy. Pedagogy* involves the science and principles of teaching children and the schooling model, whereas, *andragogy* is used to describe the principles involved in adult learning processes. Knowles summarizes four crucial insights underlying andragogy:

1. As persons mature, their self-concept changes from a dependent personality toward being self-directed.

2. Mature individuals develop a reservoir of experience that becomes an increasingly rich resource for learning.
3. The readiness of people to learn becomes oriented to the tasks of their social roles.
4. As people mature, their time perspective changes from postponed application of knowledge to immediate application and their learning shifts from subject centered to performance centered.[9]

When we speak of traditional education, subject centeredness, the schooling model and pedagogy and andragogy, it is not that one is good and one is bad. Both are appropriate in given teaching/learning situations and should be used accordingly. TEE fits into the andragogy model because it is training adult leaders who are functioning in their ministries.[10] It is preparing leaders in ministry and not for ministry. In the next chapter we will consider the components that make up a TEE program.

---

[1] Elliston, *Theological Education by Extension* 121.
[2] Personal Notes.
[3] Ibid.
[4] Winter, personal notes.
[5] Vergil Gerber, *Discipling Through TEE*, 15.
[6] Guatemala Center for Studies in TEE ministry, Occasional Paper No. 8, 28.
[7] Elliston, *Theological Education by Extension* 121-122.
[8] Ibid, 67-68.
[9] Ibid, 69.
[10] Ibid, 69.

5

COMPONENTS OF THEOLOGICAL EDUCATION BY EXTENSION

When we speak of the components of Theological Education by Extension, we refer to the essential elements in a good TEE program that will fulfill the goals for this type of leadership training. Before considering these components, we want to mention some general observations of how the extension center works.

"The built-in flexibility of the extension seminary allows students on many levels to study for the ministry."[1]

The requirements for an extension center include the following:

1. Students. This means that the center will be where the students already are since the purpose is further preparation for those who are in the ministry.

2. Teachers, monitors, or coordinators of the local center. These center leaders are of primary importance. Without them the centers will not function. They need to be people who have the vision, conviction, and capability to disciple others.

3. Self-teaching materials. Perhaps it depends on the level of training desired as to whether self-teaching materials are the only way. We know of centers where inductive studies are used and others where textbooks and notebooks are used.

4. Transportation for professors. If the teachers live far away and are not local, transportation and expense becomes a problem. Wagner quotes Peter Savage on the problem of not conducting a weekly seminar.

> Frankly, through many experiments, I have come back to the same conclusion that the regular weekly visit of the teacher every two weeks do approximately the same amount of work as the students meeting the teacher every week. Furthermore the rote learning system is so ingrained in them that many of the cognate skill areas such as analysis and application are not within their reach without the more frequent presence of the teacher.[2]

5. Classrooms. Of course, this can be expensive if a "formal" extension center is set up. Meeting in churches or homes is much less expensive.

6. Furniture. There is need of a blackboard, tables, chairs, bookcases, etc.; but this also depends on where the seminar session is held.

7. Schedule. The students and professor or monitor must agree upon the schedule. There is great flexibility here.

8. Placement examinations. Each ethnic group or culture should develop its own placement exams in order to decide the self-instructional materials to be used.

9. Functional library. For students in a diploma-level program or above there is need of a library with concordances, Bible dictionaries, commentaries, several versions of the Bible, and other research materials. This is a difficult problem in some TEE centers. Sometimes, if the pastor is involved in the program, he will have a personal partial library.

10. Secretary. This would be needed in a larger, more "formal" center, whereas normally the coordinator would be able to handle this need.[3]

The three components of TEE are very well illustrated by Ted Ward's *Split-Rail Fence Analogy* and Fred Holland's *Two-Track Analogy* as given by Edgar Elliston in his ML540 syllabus.[4]

Figure 2

Ward's Split-Rail Fence Analogy

Introduction   Ted Ward of Trinity Theological Seminary was
greatly used of God in the early days of
Theological Education by Extension (TEE). He
traveled extensively along with Sam Rowen holding
seminars and explaining TEE to many different
trainers. The split-rail fence analogy was used to
point out how the learning elements of TEE took
place. The model was a good model and easily
grasped. Remember the model should be interpreted
in the TEE context.

Basic Analogy

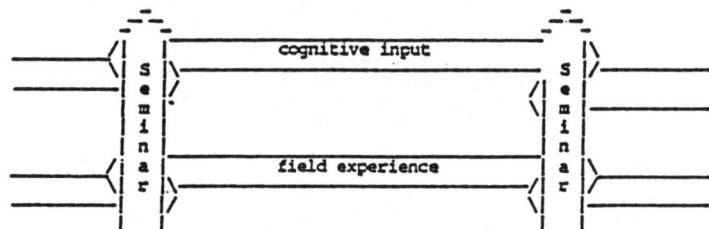

Explanation of terms

Term	Explanation
Cognitive input	Cognitive input referred to the information being learned in the TEE programs. This information for the most part was packaged in self study formats (programmed instruction, workbooks, etc.)
Field experience	Field experience referred to the application of what was being learned by the student in the local ministry context of which the student was a part. The student, living in his/her normal living context, was expected to use the things being learned in the local church situation.
Seminars	Seminars referred to the group meetings which centered around dynamic interaction over the information being learned through self-study. Through the seminar competent teachers would use the time to clarify, apply, motivate, facilitate praxilogical reflection, and stimulate the students to continue their self-study. A major purpose of the seminars was to insure that the students were actually applying the learning to the field experience and learning from not only the cognitive input but reflecting on the experience as well.

Figure 3

Holland's Two-Track Analogy

Introduction   Fred Holland modified the basic Split-rail Fence
Analogy to include a vital element of learning very
important in leadership--that of spiritual
formation. He borrowed the term from Catholic
Educators. The basic description of formation
given by Holland as understood by Catholic training
institutions is given in the quote below.

> Formation is considered to be the process by
> which the student-candidate for the ministry
> is influenced and directed in spiritual growth
> and development. Every Catholic institution
> for theological training has a spiritual
> director who is responsible for the care of
> the souls and conduct of the students. While
> formation may seem to regiment spiritual
> activities, it does help to develop needed
> devotional habits (Holland 1978:8).

Basic Analogy

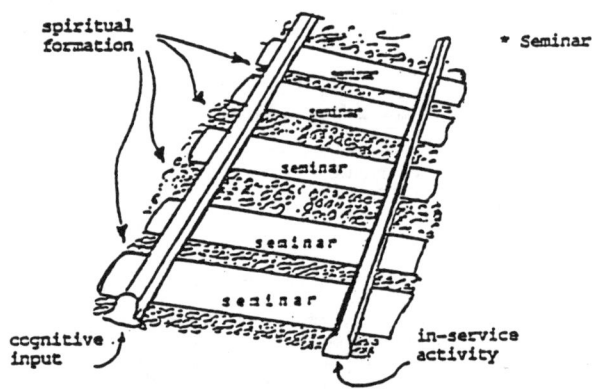

Explanation of Terms

Term	Explanation
Cognitive input	Same as Split-rail Fence Analogy
In-service activity	Same as field experience in Split-rail Fence Analogy
Spiritual formation	Basically a protestant application of the description of formation given above in the quote
Seminar	Same as seminar in Split-rail Fence Analogy

As seen in these analogies, the three components of TEE are as follows:

1. Programmed Instruction (PI). This is the *Cognitive Input*, the information being learned. This information has been packaged in PI self-study books or in workbooks.
2. In-service or *Field Experience*, refers to the application of what is learned by the student in practical ministry in the local church.
3. *Seminar Sessions*. These are group meetings centered around dynamic interaction over information learned through self-study. The coordinator or teacher tries to clarify, motivate, facilitate, reflect, and stimulate the students. He is the key for success at the local TEE center.

In this chapter we will consider the second and third components first, and in the following chapter the cognitive input.

The bottom rail of Ward's split-rail fence is *field* (or in-service) *experience*. Of course, this learning is the real purpose of the cognitive input. Learning is sometimes defined as a change in behavior. W. James Popham and Eva I. Baker write, "Instructional decisions . . . are based on what happens to the learners as consequences of instruction."[5] The purpose is for those studying should put into practice what is learned in their lives and ministries. Remember the apprenticeship system! Remember the in-service training!

Yes, the purpose of instruction is a changed life and a growing ministry, it is to "grow in grace and in the knowledge of our Lord and Savior Jesus Christ" (II Peter 3:18, KJV). It is learning in order to disciple disciplers. It is committing to faithful men that which they will be able to teach others. It is "making disciples of all nations." Wagner writes, "Most folk working in extension agree that if theological training does not result in growing churches, it is not fulfilling its basic purpose."[6]

This purpose is what makes the cognitive input so valuable and also emphasizes the great importance of the weekly seminar session and its leader.

C. Peter Wagner gives an example of a hypothetical class session.

> Each class session has several objectives. First the professor uses about ten minutes to give an examination on the materials the students have been studying the previous week. Twenty minutes is used for a discussion of the answers to the test, providing the students immediate feedback, twenty-five minutes for a general discussion and application of the previous week's work with the students raising any problems they might have run into, and the final five minutes going over the assignment for the following week.[7]

Another way to express the importance of the weekly seminar session is to consider a time schedule or order schedule for the use of the time allotted. After the leader or coordinator of the group prepares and plans well, he would apply the following schedule:

1. Arrive on time, greet and talk with the people. It is better to be early than late! Fellowship with the students is very important.
2. At the beginning of the session a chorus may be sung or a short devotional may be given.
3. A short prayer time may be had, praying for *their needs*.
4. Mark attendance and collect fees, etc. This can be the responsibility of another person, such as the coordinator.
5. A short quiz may be given on the assignment studied.

6. Check to see that the text responses have been filled in.
7. A brief review of the lesson should be given.
8. The *Seminar Discussion.* This is the most important part of the "round-table discussion." The leader tries to get total participation. This is where the problem solving level of learning takes place. One great challenge here is that the leader has a goal of speaking only 30% of the time in leading this discussion.
9. Sum up the discussion and make the application.
10. Look for the spiritual needs of the group.
11. Look for the academic needs in the group.
12. Introduce the next week's lesson.
13. Closing prayer. Pray for application in the lives and ministries of the students.
14. Be available to the people.

We have said that in our experience with TEE in Brazil, Mexico, and Guatemala, the coordinator of these "leaders in ministry" is the most important person to inspire and give vision to the group and encourage them to study. This can be a fulfillment of II Timothy 2:2: "And the things you have heard me say in the presence of many witnesses entrust to reliable men who will also be qualified to teach others" (NIV).

But let's return to Ward's analogy of the Split-Rail Fence. Because of the importance of the bottom rail of the fence (*field experience)* and the importance of the posts that hold up the fence (weekly *seminar sessions),* we see what a vital place the top rail, or *cognitive input,* has on the study. Cognitive input refers to the materials we use for study. We now consider this component in the following chapter.

---

[1] Covell, 84.
[2] Covell, 96.

---

[3] Covell, 90-91.
[4] Elliston, 80-82.
[5] W. James Popham and Eva I. Baker, *Establishing Instructional Goals*, 11.
[6] Wagner, 97.
[7] Ibid

6

COMPONENTS OF TEE: PROGRAMMED INSTRUCTION (PI)

Programmed Instruction is a progressive method to furnish the cognitive input. Programming was introduced by Ted Ward in 1969. The texts are autodidactic, self-teaching. The text is the teacher and all the necessary information is within the text. Some object to a strictly programmed text as too repetitive. Therefore, semi-programmed textbooks were introduced. These have the added element of open-ended questions that would be the main focus of the discussion in the center classes. The texts used are divided into three parts: *information* repeated several times (usually given as a frame), the *answer* given by the student to the information given, and a *reward* or approval of a correct answer. If the student gives the right answer, he/she is immediately rewarded; if his/her answer is wrong, he/she is immediately corrected. It is helpful to consider seven criteria or characteristics of programmed instruction:

1. It is instructional material. It is not a test or a series of questions.
2. It has specific objectives which it aims to meet.
3. It is developed empirically. Program structure—content, sequence, step size and format—is a

synthesis of the programmer's assumptions and feedback obtained from students.

4. It is self-instructional. Its contents need not be explained, reviewed, or repeated neither by other instructional materials nor by an instructor.

5. It is self-pacing. It need not be limited by time constraints such as a 50-minute class period, by a group presentation device such as a movie, nor by student group characteristics, e.g., a "slow" student will not hold back the others.

6. It requires students to solve problems or make discriminations as they proceed through the instructional material.

7. It requires increasingly complex behavior of the student as he/she progresses through it. Each step leads to and contributes to new behaviors in subsequent frames. Repetition and isolated "review" frames are not essential. Review is handled by gradual addition of complexity.

The following diagram illustrates some of the aspects of PI. The following *Notes on Programmed Instruction*[1] are helpful in understanding how PI works and of what it consists.

Figure 4

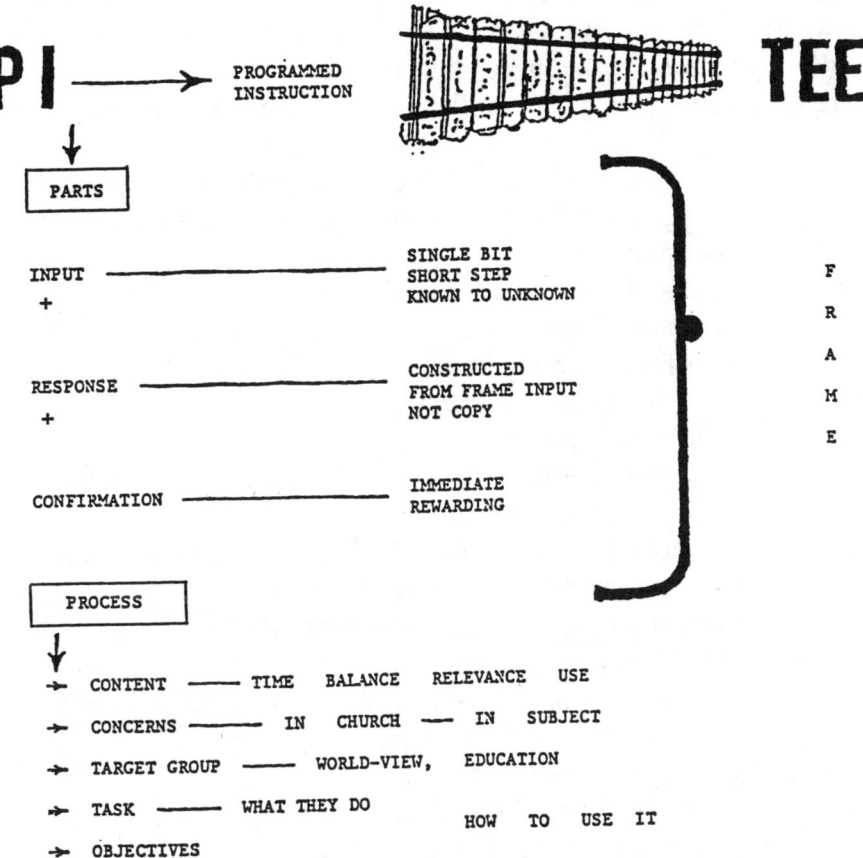

The objective of all dedicated missionaries should be to thoroughly analyze all situations, anticipate all problems prior to their occurrence, have answers for these problems, and move swiftly to solve them when called upon to do so. However, when you are up to your knickers in alligators, it is difficult to remind yourself that your initial objective was to drain the swamp.

The idea is—if you don't know where you are going, how are you going to know when you get there? Some goals and objectives should:

Be stated in measurable terms.

Be a single item.

Be affective or cognitive yet still have overt
indicators.

Be stated in behavior terms.

Be stated in terms of motor performance, verbal, and
discrimination.

Have conditions stated—what, when, where, and how.

Have standards—time limit, accuracy, etc.

Have sub-objectives—a part of the whole
broken into steps or parts.

Have interim objectives—learning steps that fall away
as the skill is learned.

Goals for preparing objectives:

1. Set out general objectives:

Related to the subject matter

Important to the student

Job related and performance rated

2. Identify specific behaviors:

What is to be done

Under what conditions

With what level of proficiency

Fuzzy objectives are to know, understand, really understand, appreciate, fully appreciate, believe, enjoy etc.

More precise objectives are to write, recite, identify, solve, and construct.

A good program takes over certain functions of the teacher. It leads the student through a carefully designed, controlled series of learning experiences which achieve behavioral-stated specific objectives.

Seven principles in PI are:

1. ASSOCIATION

   The pretest shows you where the learner is—his/her starting place. Small steps in a program lead progressively from known to unknown.

2. ACTIVE RESPONSE

   Program speaks to student and student responds to program. The student's response is elicited by the program, not just questions and blanks to fill in.

3. APPROACH ATTITUDE

   Add environment or exposure level material.

4. RELEVANCE

   Have clear objectives which are job and culture related.

5. REINFORCEMENT

   Knowledge of results, given immediately, reinforces learning. Feedback may correct errors, but try to avoid the possibility of error.

6. LEARNER RATE

   Material must be of the proper level. Learner will cover the lesson at his/her own rate.

7. RETENTION

   This is aided by the association of unknown to known. It is also aided by immediate use. The frame response must use, not repeat the input. (Copy frames do not aid retention.)

A program is made up of frames. A frame is made up of INPUT-RESPONSE-CONFIRMATION. The input may be given as:

1. Information—statement of fact or introduction.
2. A generalization of the first given concept.
3. Discrimination of the given fact from another.
4. Illustration, story, or example.
5. Practice material.
6. Review or revision.
7. Rule and example of its operation.
8. Release frame, criterion test frame, or final question.

The response may:

1. Require an answer to a direct question.
2. Ask yes or no.
3. Require students to given an example.
4. Ask why this is true.
5. Give part of the answer and ask students for another part.
6. Ask for an opinion. (Avoid multiple choice, true and false, and fill-in-the-blanks with new learners/readers.)

The confirmation may be given as:

1. A direct answer.
2. An expansion of possible answers if a broad question is asked. (Remember if you ask why they think something, they are never wrong.)
3. The part of the lesson that has the answer.

About people stealing answers:

1. They shouldn't have to—use good, short-step PI.
2. Build the answer into the next frame, so the student has to read the next frame to get his/her confirmation.

3. Explain to the student the value of honesty. He/She will learn better and enjoy the lesson more. He/She will be better prepared for the exam.

Levels of learning:
1. Exposure
2. Recognition
3. Recall
4. Memory
5. Concept

There are three main steps to setting up a program.
1. Preparation
   Select a subject (research to see if there already is a program that can be used, or that can be adapted to your needs).
   General statement—deals with scope of content, skills desired, extra concerns.
   General objectives—content or job related.
   Content analysis—breaks it into broad themes, fitting and changing it to meet your needs.
   Define entering skills—assumptions are usually wrong.
   Design criterion test.
2. Writing
   Introduction—approach attitude
   Review of concepts
   Development of concepts
   Criterion frames
   Summary and tests
3. Testing and revision
   Test small parts—change until it works.
   Test for level of mastery with target group testee.
   Validation—the proving of the complete program in a field situation.

Some early problems in programming are:
1. Lack of content depth.
2. Need for involvement with Scriptures—words, exegesis.
3. Lack of sticking to objective—writing only.
4. Lack of flow—frame to frame, section to section, to terminal frame and then day to day building—review—teaching three things (give one, then two, review 1, 2, 3).
5. Need single bit frames—not just short.
6. Keep subject in mind—overall objectives.
7. Teach—you don't teach by telling everything in one frame.

Suggested writing process:
1. Write terminal frame first.
2. Begin—this lesson is about . . .
3. Take steps leading to the objective.
4. Give revision—practice on all concepts.
5. Don't ramble—move logically through lesson.
6. Have a daily objective - work out a source - response table.
7. Responses must involve people with materials.
8. Get into the content of your materials.
9. *Not* essays on the theme of your materials.

In these notes we are faced with educational goals and objectives. These thoughts bring us to a consideration of taxonomies. "A *taxonomy* is an ordered arrangement of data into identifiable categories in which the criterion is based on relationships inherent in the data itself."[2] Some of the famous taxonomies are Bloom's *Taxonomy of Cognitive Domain*, Krathwohle's *Taxonomy of Affective Domain*, and Simpson's

Taxonomy of Psychomotor Domain. Here's an example of Bloom's Taxonomy as applied to TEE.
1. Knowledge
    What is TEE? Give a definition. Where did the TEE concept begin and under what circumstances?
2. Comprehension
    In your opinion, why is TEE an important concept for theological training in Third-World countries?
3. Application
    How can the TEE concept be used right now in your present ministry in church or mission?
4. Analysis
    Can you identify and define the relationships that exist in a good program of TEE? What are the relationships and components?
5. Synthesis
    Create a new form of TEE that would be applicable to adults with less than a second grade education. Consider culture in your project. Draw a chart of possible extension programs.
6. Evaluation
    What do you feel are the advantages and disadvantages of TEE as contrasted with residential training? What are your reasons and how would you evaluate your existing or proposed "center"?

Programmed and semi-programmed textbooks were used quite early in TEE. A strictly programmed book gives no opportunity for individual response. The semi-programmed textbook provides open-ended questions as the main focus of the discussions in the center classes. Some believe that programmed instruction is too simplistic for intensive biblical studies. The textbooks are still being used very effectively throughout the world in leadership training.

But how does PI work? What are the principles of programmed learning? The following is an example of how the program works. There is *information, response,* and *confirmation.* The answers are on the last page. These frames will teach the five steps of programming. Try it![3]

PRINCIPLES OF PROGRAMMED LEARNING

1. Learning should be fun. However, in the early stages, students often make many errors. Most people (do/do not) like to make errors.
2. When a student makes many errors in learning, he/she often decides that he/she does not like the subject. He/She would be more correct to decide that he/she does not like to make

   _____.
3. For a long time, educators, psychologists, and people in general thought it was impossible to learn without making a large number of errors. In fact, they even had a name for this kind of learning. They called it "trial-and-
   _____" learning.
4. Recent developments in the psychology of learning have cast serious doubts as to the necessity of "trial-and-error" learning. If the learning material is carefully prepared or *programmed,* in a special way, the student can master the subject while making very few errors. The material you are reading right now has been prepared, or _____ in this special way.
5. The basic idea of programmed learning is that the most efficient, pleasant, and permanent learning takes place when the student proceeds through a programmed course by a

large number of small, easy-to-take steps. If each step the student takes is small, he/she (is/is not) likely to make errors.

6. A *programmed course* is made up of many small, easy-to-take steps. A student can proceed from knowing very little about a subject to mastery of the subject by going through a _____. If the programmed course is carefully prepared, he/she should make (many/few) errors along the way.

7. Programmed learning has many features which are different from conventional methods of learning. You have already learned one of these principles. This principle is that a student learns best if he/she proceeds by small _____.

8. The features of programmed learning are applications of learning principles discovered in psychological laboratories. You have learned the first of these principles. You can guess that we call it the Principle of Small _____.

9. The principles on which programmed learning is based were discovered in (psychological/astrological) laboratories. The first step of these principles is the Principle of Small Steps.

10. The first Principle of Programmed Learning is the *Principle of* _____ _____.

11. What is the first Principle of Programmed Learning?

_____ _____ _____

_____ _____.

12. Another finding from the psychological laboratories is that the student learns best if he/she actively responds as he/she is learning. The student who actually works out algebra problems will probably do (better/worse) on a test than the student who only reads the explanations and looks at the examples.

13. Another way to say that people "learn by doing" is to say

that they learn by *active responding*. You can guess that the second Principle of Programmed Learning is the Principle of Active _____.

14. Principles of Programmed Learning:
    a. The Principle of Small Steps
    b. The Principle of _____
    _____.

15. Principles of Programmed Learning:
    a. The Principle of _____
    _____.
    b. The Principle of _____
    _____.

16. Principles of Programmed Learning:
    a. _____ _____
    _____ _____
    _____.
    b. _____ _____
    _____ _____
    _____.

17. The third principle from the psychological laboratory: Students learn best when they can *confirm* their answers immediately. A student who must wait two weeks for test results probably (will/will not) learn as well as a student whose test is scored immediately.

18. Third Principle: A student learns best when he/she can *confirm* his/her answers immediately. This can be called the Principle of Immediate Confirmation. In the programmed course you are now using, you can confirm your answers immediately. So this programmed course (does/does not) use the Principle of Immediate _____.

19. When a student can immediately confirm his/her answer, the Principle of _____ _____ is being applied.

20. Three learning principles:

    a. The Principle of Small _____.

    b. The Principle of Active _____.

    c. The Principle of Immediate _____.

21. Three learning principles:

    a. The Principle of _____

      _____.

    b. The Principle of _____

      _____.

    c. The Principle of _____

      _____.

22. When a subject matter, such as calculus, is broken down into parts so that the student can easily go from one item to the next, we are using the Principle of _____ _____.

23. When the material from which the student is learning demands that he/she write his/her answer out, the Principle of _____ _____ is being used.

24. When the learning material is arranged so that the student can find out immediately if his/her answer is correct or incorrect, the Principle of _____ _____ is being used.

25. Some people naturally learn more rapidly or more slowly than others. If the pace of a classroom is too fast or too slow for a child, he/she probably (will/will not) learn as well as he/she could at his/her own pace.

26. In programmed learning, each student can work each step as slowly or as quickly as he/she chooses. This is called the Principle of Self-Pacing. Since you can spend as much or as little time as you wish on each step in this course, the Principle of Self-Pacing (is/is not) being used.

27. The Principle of Programmed Learning which allows each student to *pace* himself is called the Principle of _____-_____.

28. When each student is allowed to learn at his/her own rate (as with a private tutor), the Principle of _____-_____ is being used.

29. You have now learned four of the five most important principles of programmed learning. Now we will review them.
    a. Principle of _____ _____ (easy sequence of steps).
    b. Principle of _____ _____ (student learns immediately right or wrong).
    c. Principle of _____ _____ (student can choose his/her speed).
    d. Principle of _____-_____ (student can choose his/her speed).

30. In programmed learning, the student makes a complete record of his/her learning experience. If he/she writes down his/her answer to each step, it (is/is not) possible to find out exactly where he/she made mistakes.

31. Suppose a student goes through 100 steps in a programmed course and writes down each answer. He/She makes four mistakes. From his/her record you (can/cannot) tell where each mistake was made.

32. Suppose you want to improve a programmed course by revising it. Suppose ten students all make a mistake on step number thirty-seven. This probably (would/would not) be a good frame to revise.

33. Students miss steps because they are too big, unclear, or have not been reviewed often enough. By looking over a programmed course, you (can/cannot) see exactly what steps came before a step on which a mistake was made.

34. Since accurate records of the learning experience of each student are available, revisions can be made on the basis of actual student responses. If the presentation of some point

is not clear, this (will/will not) show up in the student's performance on the programmed course.

35. Revision of a programmed course on the basis of student performance is called the Principle of Program Testing. Since the course you are taking now has been developed on this basis, the Principle of _____ _____ has been used here.

36. Making revisions of programmed courses on the basis of the learning records of students is making use of the fifth Programming Principle, _____ _____ _____ _____ _____.

37. Now we will review them.
    a. Principle of _____ _____
       (easy progress from item to item)
    b. Principle of _____ _____
       (student actively records his/her response)
    c. Principle of _____ _____
       (rapid knowledge of correctness)
    d. Principle of _____-_____
       (student chooses speed of progress)
    e. Principle of _____ _____
       (program revised on basis performance)

38. Now see if you can list five programming principles without hints.
    a. _____
    b. _____
    c. _____
    d. _____
    e. _____

39. A student "gives up" on an algebra lesson from his/her textbook because the steps in the first problem are much too big. What programming principle was not followed here?

_____

40. A student takes an examination. The teacher, by working late each night, gets the papers graded in one week and returns them to the class. The student has since lost interest and doesn't check his/her paper. What programming principle has not been followed?_____

41. A student goes through a programmed course writing down his/her response to every step. What programming principle is being followed here?_____

42. A programmer finds that on the first draft of a programmed course students made over 50% errors. He/She completely revises the course. In the new version, students make only 4% errors. What programming principle has been used here?

43. A very bright student becomes bored because he/she already knows the material being taught. As a result he/she daydreams and gets into trouble with his/her teacher. What programming principle has not been used here?

44. A student is convinced by previous experience that he/she cannot learn algebra. He/She happens to try a programmed course in algebra. To his/her surprise, he/she gets to find that each of the first seventy-five steps he/she tries are easy to understand and he/she has no difficulty. What programming principle is being used here?

45. A good teacher is disturbed because students are not "getting" the material. They say they don't understand his/her lectures or the textbook. Unfortunately, he/she has no specific record of what goes wrong, so he/she has difficulty in revising and improving his/her presentation. What programming principle is not being followed here?

46. A student is studying chemical equations. He/She thinks he/she "understands" but never actually practices any equations out. He/She takes a test on chemical equations and gets a very low score. What programming principle is not being followed here? _____

47. A student is learning physics from a programmed course. He/She is not absolutely sure of every answer, but he/she can check each answer within a second after he/she writes it. What programming principle is being followed here?

_____

48. A very careful student is learning electronics from a programmed course. It takes him twice as long to finish as it takes the rest of the class. However, on the final test, he/she does as well as anyone. What programming principle has been followed here? _____

49. It is easy to remember the five Principles of Programmed Learning. To do this, just remember what happens as you go through a programmed course. The first thing you do is *read* the material in a step. This material has been carefully constructed so that you can take that step easily. Therefore, the Principle of _____
_____ is used.

50. READ/WRITE After you READ the Small Step material, you WRITE your answer. Since writing is an active response, you are using the Principle of
_____.

51. READ/WRITE/CHECK
   a. Read Small Step material.
   b. Write your answer. Next, you CHECK your answer immediately. Since you can find out immediately if

your answer is correct, you are using the Principle of _____ _____ .

52. READ/WRITE/CHECK/ADVANCE   After reading, writing, and checking your answer, you ADVANCE to the next step as slowly or as quickly as you wish. Since you can advance at your own rate, you are using the Principle of _____ - _____ .

53. To remember the first four Principles of Programmed Learning, just remember what happens when you work through a programmed course.
    a. READ: This reminds you that you first read the specially-constructed material in each step. So the first programming principle is the Principle of

    _____ _____ .

54. READ/WRITE/CHECK/ADVANCE
    b. WRITE: Responding to each step by writing reminds you of the Principle of _____

    _____ .

55. READ/WRITE/CHECK/ADVANCE
    c. CHECK: Being able to check each answer right away reminds you of the Principle of _____

    _____ .

56. READ/WRITE/CHECK/ADVANCE
    d. ADVANCE: Being able to take each step at your own rate reminds you of the Principle of _____

    _____ .

57. READ/WRITE/CHECK/ADVANCE
    Remember the order of events as you go through a programmed course. These will help you remember the first four principles of programming. Review.
    a. Principle of _____ _____
    b. Principle of _____ _____

    c. Principle of _____ _____

    d. Principle of _____ -_____

58. To remember the fifth and most important Principle of Programmed Learning, remember this word: RECORD. This will remind you that the detailed record which the student makes provides for revising the programmed course. This reminds   you   of   the   Principle   of

_____ _____.

59. READ/WRITE/CHECK/ADVANCE/RECORD

    By remembering these five key words, you can easily remember the five important features of programmed learning.

    a. Principle of _____ _____

    b. Principle of _____ _____

    c. Principle of _____ _____

    d. Principle of _____ _____

    e. Principle of _____ _____

PRINCIPLES OF PROGRAMMED LEARNING
Answer Sheet

1. do not
2. errors
3. error
4. programmed
5. is not
6. programmed course/few
7. steps
8. steps
9. psychological
10. small steps
11. the principle of small steps
12. better
13. responding
14. active responding
15. small steps/active responding
16. principle of small steps/principle of active responding
17. will not
18. does/confirmation
19. immediate confirmation
20. steps/ response/ confirmation
21. small steps/ active responding/ immediate confirmation
22. small steps
23. active responding
24. immediate confirmation
25. will not
26. is
27. self-pacing
28. self-pacing
29. small steps/active responding/immediate confirmation/self-pacing
30. is

31. can
32. would
33. can
34. will
35. program testing
36. the principle of program testing
37. small steps/active responding/immediate confirmation/self-pacing/program testing
38. principle of small steps/principle of active responding/principle of immediate confirmation/principle of self-pacing/principle of program testing
39. the principle of small steps
40. the principle of immediate confirmation
41. the principle of active responding
42. the principle of program testing
43. the principle of self-pacing
44. the principle of small steps
45. the principle of program testing
46. the principle of active responding
47. the principle of immediate confirmation
48. the principle of self-pacing
49. small steps
50. active responding
51. immediate confirmation
52. self-pacing
53. small steps
54. active responding
55. immediate confirmation
56. self-pacing
57. small steps/active responding/immediate confirmation/self-pacing
58. program testing
59. small steps/active responding/immediate confirmation/self-pacing/program testing

Programmed or semi-programmed texts are one way of supplying cognitive input. There are other materials that can be used in TEE discipling. Some programs use inductive studies with information and questions in a text such as is common in the Navigator's series of books. Others use regular Bible school or seminary textbooks, or texts especially prepared with a separate workbook of questions and studies.

A good example of this is the FLET program. FLET (Facultad Latinoamericana de Estudios Teologicos), in cooperation with Logoi, Inc. and SEAN, is producing and using textbooks and workbooks throughout Latin America in a highly intensive program.

We have spoken of TEE as a movement and have also mentioned the training of leaders. However, is TEE a movement and who are the leaders being trained? The next chapter will consider these questions.

---

[1] Personal notes from material collected, unknown source.
[2] Elliston, *Theological Education by Extension* 63.
[3] Personal notes from material collected.

7

WHO ARE THE LEADERS IN TEE?

Throughout this paper we have spoken of the leaders in TEE, but who are these leaders? We have also spoken of TEE as a movement. Does this fit the bill? We will consider these two questions in this chapter.

When we speak of TEE, we speak of ministry in and to the whole body of Christ. We have seen from Ephesians 4 that there is to be a *discovering* and *developing* and *using* of spiritual gifts in the ministry of all the saints. This means that we find leadership at all levels of church life and ministry. There is a breakdown of the false dichotomy between clergy and laity and a fuller understanding of the priesthood of all believers. Therefore, we find God-given leadership in Sunday School classes, among elders or pastors and deacons, leaders of nurture and caring, leaders of evangelism and church planting, leaders of local and national and international organizations. In TEE we speak of "functioning leaders," those in actual ministry function. Donald McGavran in his influential book, *Understanding Church Growth*, divided church growth into five classes of leaders. Lois McKinney later modified this idea to describe different levels of leaders that needed to be trained with different kinds of training. There are five types of leadership being trained:

Type 1—local leaders in rural or city churches.
Type 2—overseers of small congregations in rural or city areas.
Type 3—overseers of larger congregations or clusters of small congregations in rural or city areas.
Type 4—regional, national, or international administrators.
Type 5—research/influence leaders such as: strategists, theologians, national evangelists.[1]

Edgar J. Elliston has given us much help in expanding these concepts. He writes,

I am suggesting that these types of leaders may be interpreted more broadly to interpret influence needs or functions in the Church. Each type of leader may also be differentiated on the basis of the ways the attributes of power, such as comprehensiveness, intensity and extensiveness are employed in the influence process. . . . "Comprehensiveness" refers to the range of lifestyle issues. "Intensity" refers to the depth to which these issues are addressed. "Extensiveness" refers to a person's sphere of influence.[2]

The following table by Elliston is also helpful.[3]

Figure 5

LEADER TYPES BASIC DESCRIPTION

Type	Designation	Role	Distribution / Extensiveness	Comprehensiveness	Intensity	Equipping
T-1	non-professional, small group	Community links / primary influence	1 to 2 - 12	Potentially all of one's lifestyle issues	Potentially very high	Informal
T-2	para-professional, multiple small group	Oversight of multiple small groups	1 to 20 - 100	Potentially high	Potentially high	Nonformal
T-3	semi-professional, community	Congregational oversight	1 to 50 - 250	Moderate	moderate	Formal, e.g., Christian College, M.Div.,
T-4	professional, regional	Regional / strategic leadership	1 to 250 - 3000	Moderate to low	Moderate to low	M.A. ICS; D.Min.
T-5	professional, international	Strategic leadership across denominations	1 to 3000 - 10,000	Low	Low	Informal / nonformal

He further explains,

Each type of leader fills an important niche in the overall leadership of the church. If any type is missing, the health of the church and its potential for evangelism, nurture and service both within its own community and beyond is seriously limited. Type One leaders are better connected in the community and can better do the primary evangelism, pastoral care and nurturing through face-to-face interaction. Type Two leaders provide the primary oversight of outreach and care. They are likely to know every person they influence. Type Three leaders typically serve a congregating function for a local congregation as the pastor. They begin to influence indirectly. Types Four and Five provide broad perspective, strategic direction and deeper level instruction. They increasingly influence indirectly through other people, or other means such as publishing, mass media, denominational structures, or mission policy-making.[4]

Fred Holland gives a helpful perspective on local church leadership, his "Leader-Saint Axis." Here, we will only give the explanation of the diagram:

1. Ministries appropriate to saints—recognizes the breadth of ministry for the non-leaders (non-set-apart-leaders) in a church. The saints represent Ephesians 4:12 and show that there is overlap between functions and ministries of saints and leaders.
2. Ministries only for saints—defined as those done only by saints.
3. Ministries appropriate to leaders—described in Ephesians 4:11. This category recognizes that leader functions and ministries overlap saint functions and ministries.
4. Ministry only for leaders—God-appointed leadership in a local church.

5. Ministries for both—recognizes that each person has spiritual gifts and that leaders and saints may have the same gifts.
6. Non-ordained functions—those which should be done in order to free leaders to exercise their gifts.
7. Quasi-ordained functions—ministry functions which have been limited to ordained people but should be allowed for those who have the gifts.
8. Ordained functions—recognizes those functions which God will hold leadership accountable for.[5]

But, what is a leader? Edgar J. Elliston helps us understand leadership.

A *leader* in the biblical context for which we are interested in studying and training, is a person, with God-given capacity *and* with a God-given responsibility to influence a specific group of God's people toward God's purposes for the group.[6]

He continues to explain, "though potential leaders are born, effective leaders are made as a result of opportunity, training (formal, nonformal, or informal), and experience."[7] These concepts help us as we consider leadership training through TEE. Is TEE a movement? Elliston gives us a definition and then some vital elements that constitute a movement.

A group of people, who are organized for, ideologically motivated by, and committed to a purpose which implements some form of personal or social change, who are actively engaged in the recruitment or others; and the established order within which it originated. (CIC:371 quoting Gerlach and Hine 1970:xvi).[8]

There are many other considerations in a movement that cause social change, etc. But, we close this thought by considering five commitments needed to participate in a movement:

1. Commitment to personal involvement.

2. Commitment to persuade others to join.
3. Commitment to the beliefs and ideals of the movement.
4. Commitment to participate in flexible, nonbureaucratic cell-group organization.
5. Commitment to endure opposition and misunderstanding.

Certainly TEE has been and still is involved in all types of leadership training. Certainly TEE started as a movement across Latin America and the Third World and still has some of these elements as it continues changing attitudes and practices of theological education throughout the world. In many places it continues as a force for good in the body of Christ.

---

[1] Elliston, *Theological Education by Extension* 56.
[2] Elliston, *Developing Leaders at a Distance* 10.
[3] Ibid, 11.
[4] Ibid, 12.
[5] Elliston, *Theological Education by Extension* 61.
[6] Ibid, 46.
[7] Ibid, 48.
[8] Ibid, 50.

8

BLESSINGS AND PROBLEMS IN TEE

We have traced the birth and history of a movement, a vision and a conviction: theological education throughout the world. There is constant need for evaluation, revision, openness, and challenge as a form of nonformal education. We will consider some of the blessings and some of the problems of this continuing movement.

There are advantages and blessings in the model of TEE. Some of these include the following:

1. The training of people without cultural extraction. The "Two-Thirds" world church should be allowed to develop along its own cultural lines rather than being forced into the model of another culture.
2. The people are trained *in* ministry rather than *for* ministry. TEE trains leaders where they are and the student does not see "the better life" nor is he spoiled by it.
3. There is the training of leaders who need training and cannot obtain it through residence situations. Rapid church growth makes it impossible for training them fast enough in traditional methods.
4. Many Third World leaders are poor. TEE is one of the cheapest and best ways to educate them.

5. TEE trains many more people than will ever be trained in residence situations. This gives a better biblical perspective of the Body of Christ and the priesthood of all believers.
6. TEE provides relevant training in doing practical service for the leadership context.
7. TEE provides a flexible educational system in time considerations, teaching situations, and role applications.

But, TEE is not a panacea, and there are weaknesses. Mulholland listed some of these weaknesses which were pointed out in a workshop in Cochabamba, Bolivia, in 1975. Some of these weaknesses continue and continually need to be confronted:

1. Failure of students to complete assignments. There needs to be continual awareness in the weekly seminar session to see if the students are doing their homework.
2. Inadequate programmed materials. This problem has been alleviated to a large degree, and there are excellent materials available as well as continued production of materials.
3. Lack of teachers trained in the use of programmed learning materials. This is true and a constant challenge. We hold workshops to help in this area of need.
4. Lack of programmed textbooks prepared by nationals. This continues to be a vital need.
5. Lack of culturally adapted materials. This also is a continuing need although writers are conscious of this and try to write from cultural perspectives.
6. Cross-cultural problems in the areas of communication and understanding between teacher and students. This may be true where missionaries are involved with

nationals, but if the coordinators/leaders are nationals this should be lessened.

7. Lack of identification of the extension teacher with the students. This would be true if the teacher is traveling in from the outside. But, if he is "one of them," this should be alleviated.

8. Lack of sufficient theological preparation on the part of the teachers. This is and can be a problem. The teacher, indeed, should have a better preparation than those he is guiding, although he himself can be one of the learning group.

9. The extended time in order to graduate. Yes, this is a great problem, and many can become discouraged even though we try to teach them a philosophy of lifetime, on-going, continuous education.

10. The high subsidy necessary to maintain the program. This is true. We try to have the students only pay for their books which means that traveling, postage, promotion, and books must be subsidized.[1]

Elliston mentions some additional problems that continue to confront the TEE model of theological education.

1. A general unacceptance of the TEE method as equivalent training—it is usually thought of as a lay training, an improved type of correspondence course.

2. Failure to recognize TEE as a legitimate track to ordination—not accredited.

3. Failure to have dynamic interaction in the seminars which adequately deals with experiential learning and spiritual formation.

4. Failure to integrate courses into ministry experience.

5. Increasing pressure to formalize.[2]

These are legitimate concerns and must continually be faced. There must be teaching about the very significant difference between correspondence courses and TEE. The first is in the broad sphere of Christian education, while TEE is in the narrow sphere of discipleship of leaders. Dynamic interaction is very important and is the responsibility of the coordinator. There is need for better teaching of the coordinators. Yes, there is always pressure to formalize that must be resisted if the TEE program is to remain flexible and continue to meet needs of the local, cultural situation.

Is TEE alive and well? It is always a challenge to improve the TEE method, the materials, the ministry experience, and the seminars. In talking with Ted Ward and Edgar Elliston some time ago, they assured me that, yes, TEE is alive and constantly needs review and evaluation. They assure me that in India and China it is a great blessing to the ministry and helps in church growth. I myself observed that the movement is a continued blessing throughout Mexico and into Guatemala, and wherever the TEE centers function there is blessing in changed lives and in growing ministry outreach.

---

[1] Elliston, 122.
[2] Elliston, 122-123.

9

TEE 2001!

And how is Theological Education by Extension doing today? We would conclude our study by including these words of information and testimony from far and wide! Yes, TEE is alive and well and continues to be a great blessing for leadership training and discipleship in the Body of Christ worldwide.

Mexico

John Forcey from Oaxaca writes:

Oaxaca is one of the poorest states in Mexico. It is also the most indigenous. The state is fragmented politically, ethnically, and physically. Many rural poor do not speak Spanish, and education levels generally are low and economic resources are limited.

In this context TEE is a viable option for those who wish to study. When properly understood and administered, TEE makes quality training available to those who most need it. About 200 students are currently active under the Tecate Mission TEE program in Oaxaca.

Even when all of these conditions are met there is no guarantee of success in terms of a high rate of graduating students, but student testimonies in current Oaxaca classes attest to the fact that many of those currently studying could prepare themselves in no other way for greater participation in fulfilling the Lord's command to evangelize and teach.

Roland Rose from Chiapas writes:

Theological Education by Extension is operational in the southern Mexico/Guatemala border area in various forms with different denominations and missions. As practiced by the undersigned, the Regional Coordinator of Tecate Mission (a small interdenominational faith mission located in Tecate, CA) for this area, the study groups are usually church based, each having its own local coordinator in charge of all aspects of organization, teaching and administration.

The people are *campesinos*, simple country folk, mostly supporting themselves at a subsistence level (except for the young people who have left...to work...in the United States). The majority are also evangelicals..

From one small church in Canibalillo Grande have come four sterling TEE coordinators in Tecate Mission's TEE program. Froilan (age 29 and married) and Salatiel (age 32 and single) Lopez Valazquez are brothers. Oscar Valazquez Gomez (age 36 and married) is their uncle. Efrain Mejia Vazquez is a bosom friend (age 40 and married). The three family members each have only a primary education, but all have received a three-year diploma from the Instituto Biblico "Berea", now located in Huehuetenango, Guatemala. Efrain has nine years of secular education and completed a TEE program at the Presbyterian Seminary in Tapachula, Chiapas.

Salatiel has stayed at home, and has raised up a twenty student TEE group in the Canibalillo Grande church (there is only one). Froilan is pastoring a small church in Aldea El Rodeo, Cuilco, Huehuetenango, Guatemala, another border town about twenty miles northeast of Canibalillo Grande, where he has a small group of six students, and another group of twelve in Col. Las Salinas, Municipio de Chicomuselo, Chiapas, twenty miles away. Efrain has a three student group in Tuicoche, Guatemala, just over the hill from Canibalillo Grande, but he also travels monthly to the Municipio of Escuintla, Chiapas (seventy miles by car or thirty miles as the crow flies), where he oversees four small groups with a total of twenty-two students in country Presbyterian churches, and in the last month he has just started a sixth group with nine students in Ojo de Aguas, Municipio of Motozintla, Chiapas, midway between Canibalillo Grande and Escuintla. Finally, Oscar left Guatemala about ten years ago, became a naturalized Mexican citizen, married a Mexican woman, and is living in the Municipio of Pijijiapan, Chiapas, where he has started six TEE centers in country Presbyterian churches with a total of about thirty-five students. What makes these men special is not only have they started a number of centers each, but they have also maintained the students studying, active and growing over almost three years. The more advanced students have completed 8-13 courses. Although some students have dropped by the way, others have been recruited.

TEE worker Kent Traylor is coordinating a TEE class in Tijuana. The group got excited to put what they were learning into practice, arranged a JESUS film showing, rented thirty chairs, and went door-to-door with invitations. Sixty came and twenty-five made decisions for Christ! Immediately, the group is starting discipleship with the new converts, using TEE books.

Brazil

Our friend, Thomas "W" Fife, whom we first met in Brazil years ago, writes:

Does TEE reach its goal? Does it produce leaders for local churches? Yes, and much more! It produces cross-cultural missionaries, as well! For example, the small congregation I pastored in Goiania, Goias, Brazil, has produced missionary families who are serving in Portugal, Spain, Mozambique and the United States, as well as single individuals who have served in Colombia, Belgium, England, and India.

North America

The following information and testimonies come from John Underwood of SEAN, Atlanta, GA. His colleagues have given permission for their quotes and materials.

Lorraine Anderson of Gordon Conwell Theological Seminary developed a program of TEE in the deaf culture. She testifies of its value in the academic journey of the deaf. She illustrates the need among the deaf and also mentions the success of her program:

Caleb had known for about fourteen years that God had called him to minister the gospel of Jesus Christ to urban people like himself. At the local club he often rubbed shoulders with folk whose futures were being duped by drug deals, drinking binges, and even cultic invasion. These were highly vulnerable people, cut off from modern-day, high-tech access to the gospel. And yet, he felt so inadequate himself. The Bible remained a hodge-podge of mystery, big words, and unanswered questions. The prospect of venturing beyond the conversational limits of basic salvation left him numb.

Thank you for inviting me to share with you my specific use of the *Compendium*, as I have been familiar with it for many years among Hearing, urban, laity. However, I felt it could be successfully employed on the graduate level with deaf students, if approached creatively and rigorously.

Darryl Davis M.S.T., former Director of the Urban Academy, New York, wrote:

In New York City, URBACAD presently has 140 students meeting in twenty-two groups. Twenty-three churches send us students. Most come from C.B. churches, although we do have a sprinkling of non-C.B. Baptists and a few Presbyterians. Our groups meet in four different languages: English, Spanish, French, and Portuguese. A C.B. church in Chinatown is translating SEAN's basic discipleship book, *Abundant Life*, into Chinese, which will give us fifth language for ministry. Our groups reflect the city as well as the churches they represent, being a part of the "gorgeous mosaic of peoples and cultures" to which our mayor David Dunkins so often refers.

One of the best things about URBACAD's ministry is the high level of commitment that our mosaic of students demonstrate. In spite of busy home, work, and church schedules, they are willing to commit themselves to a demanding combination of home study, small group participation, and active ministry. Obviously, these are people who take their Christianity seriously and who realize that they need systematic theological training to improve their effectiveness in ministry. When theological education is made available to them where they live, work, and minister, Christians respond enthusiastically.

Michael Maclachlan, St. Andrews Anglican Parish, Coopermine, North West Territory, writes:

The Gospel was brought to the Copper Eskimo about eighty years ago by Anglican missionary priests from the U.K. The word Eskimo is an Indian word meaning 'Raw Meat Eater' and some see it as pejorative; their own word 'Inuit' meaning 'The People' is preferred. The missionaries found little formalized religious feeling among the Inuit. The very severe weather conditions, their total dependence on the vagaries of hunting and fishing, the constant danger from snow, ice, water and from large animals forced them to live entirely, and precariously, in the present. If they had time to think of spirits they were inevitably things to fear. The news of a God who loved them and died for them, who forgave them and who offered them eternal life was widely accepted among them with great joy.

It is obvious that a traditional theological college is unsuitable. Most Inuit have limited literacy, or English, or formal education. Even the rising generation is producing very few high school graduates and may not do so for another generation. There are many highly competent, gifted, leaders who are well respected in their own communities and who are committed disciples of Jesus Christ with a very deep personal spirituality. Among this group there are several called to be ministers, from whom the next generation of ordained ministers should come if they can be trained and qualified.

SEAN materials have given us a developed and tested program designed in simple faith (the Foundation course, "Abundant Life"), and progresses into both good factual teaching, sound application, and background about the Scriptures (the Pastoral Theology course). It gives us a methodology that can be applied to any other portion of the Bible. The mix of background and direct Biblical input is especially useful in a culture which is as far removed as it could be from the agrarian and political world of the New Testament. No sheep, soldiers, empires nor kings and virtually no religious life lie behind the Inuit culture. These images have to be re-interpreted in terms of hunting and traveling, eating and drinking, leadership and guiding, light and dark, all very strong images for the Inuit. Because the courses are designed for programmed learning the basic facts are well established in the student's mind giving opportunity for the tutor to spend time discussing the implications. Each week the tutor learns new things that are incomprehensible in this culture because there is no experience of them, or because the language will not support the concepts. Grace, forgiveness, eternity, have no exact translations. "A sure and certain hope" is hard to grasp in a language where the future tense begins with "if" not "when"!

Africa

Jill Goodman, TEE Director, Enseignment Theologique Decentralise, Libreville, writes:

The TEE program in Gabon is a mixture of ideas, of formats, and of culture that makes it unique not only in its immediate context but also among TEE programs in Africa.

The TEE program began in French because it is the language of learning in Gabon. As the program expanded, some who had not enough education to complete the manuals in French asked if something was available for them.

In the fifteen years that TEE has functioned in Gabon, many changes have occurred in the church. When the program began, the largest church in the Alliance was less than 500 people. Now the largest church has three services with an attendance of over 4,000. TEE began in the only church in the capital city, there are now twelve TEE centers in the greater Libreville area. Five provinces in which there are now many TEE centers were not even being reached when TEE began. All these changes have affected TEE. In general the program has grown and adapted to meet the challenges.

The future of TEE in Gabon, at this point, seems limitless. There are requests every month from a church that wants a course. There are specific courses being developed not only in Gabon but also within the Alliance in French-speaking Africa to touch subjects not yet available. The National Office is going to build a permanent building on the same land as the Bible Institute in the capital city. The building will contain a production room, a conference room, an audio-visual/computer room and an office for multiple program leaders.

Philippines

In the Philippines, Ronald P. MacKinnois writes:

The Alliance Theological Education by Extension (ALL-TEE) program of the Christian and Missionary Alliance Churches of the Philippines (CAMACOP) has been operating since 1975, with its first classes held in 1976. Since that time there have been several changes in administration and/or the program itself.

With the renewed program in place, promotion of the program began afresh. The training of pastors, lady ministers, and missionaries to be Center Leaders was revised and two-day training sessions were held in many regions of the Philippines. From 1991 to early 1994 over 700 people were trained as Center Leaders. Until now less than 100 of them have actually held classes in their churches. However, the fact they have been trained, that the ALL-TEE program is gaining popularity, and that more and more students are wanting to be involved augers well for the future of the program. These leaders are trained and know what the requirements and benefits of the program are.

Tim and Carol Freeman write from the Philippines:

Bethany Fellowship Philippines, Inc.'s goal is to establish churches in rural areas where there is no evangelical work. We work on the largest island of Luzon, in the large, northern province of Isabela among Ilokano speaking peoples. Ilokano is the third largest language in the Philippines after Cebuana (24.5%) and Tagalog (24%). Ilokanos (13%) number over 8,000,000 people. Because most towns already have an established evangelical witness, Bethany has chosen to concentrate its efforts on the neglected villages. Ninety five percent of our target people are rice and corn farmers.

We went on furlough in late 1985, searching for good training materials. God arranged a "Divine Appointment" with Dr. James Emory, who was working with Missionary Internship at the time. After listening to a description of what we were seeking to accomplish through our training ministry, Dr. Emory recommended SEAN as a possible curriculum base because of its purposeful balance between *teaching* and *doing*. We secured a license form SEAN in 1986 to translate their materials into Ilokano and purchased two computers for the work.

South Africa

Gert Steyn, Director of Theological Education by Extension College in Johannesburg, South Africa, writes:

TEEC has played an increasing role in providing Diploma courses for clergy in training. For example, in 1985, thirty Methodist probationers were registered with the College, and nearly eighty in 1992. The number of Anglican students has declined from well over 100 in 1985 to about half that in 1992, while an increasing number have been registered with TEEC.

Within its first ten years, the TEE College has enabled over 5000 people throughout Southern Africa to study Theology. Since the first Diploma student graduated in 1981, thirty-nine students have successfully completed the Diploma, thirty-five the Certificate and twenty-four the Award —within the first ten years of the College.

Today the TEE College is accepted and valued as a vital part of the church's life and ministry, providing sound academic and spiritual equipment for the ministry in Southern Africa.

Asia

Joan Newton who was Asian Secretary of SEAN International gives the following observations:

We have recently heard of one pastor who had become proud, hardened and extremely difficult to work with, who has begun this course. When he did not appear for his meal, his wife sent to his study to see what was wrong and found him broken and weeping before the Lord. He has been a new man and pastor since then.

Another greatly discouraged and rather unwillingly agreed to enroll for a SEAN course. "His whole life has changed; he simply came alive" is the comment of his tutor.

A church in Maharashtra, India, was spiritually dead, and more concerned with building programs than any ministry at all. As members began to study the SEAN courses, there was a change in the church, which became spiritually alive and dynamically involved in ministry.

Those who attended the first workshop in India, to learn how to use the material, were all graduates of a Bible school or seminary. Their enthusiasm was most rewarding! They found that, although the material is simple, they were learning things in those few days that they had not learned in their seminary training. For example, they had not been taught basic methods of Bible study . . . observing, interpreting and then applying its truths. They also recognized that this Matthew course (only one of the six books was available at the time) with its Leader's Manual was a valuable tool in training others. All those in this workshop became actively involved; some trained others to lead groups, now many students have graduated having completed all six books . . . and, incidentally, more are coming to Christ in the area as God's people are motivated to serve.

Papua New Guinea

David Rowsome from Christian Leaders Training College (CLTC) in Papua New Guinea writes:

The latest edition of Operation World describes TEE as "one of the significant missiological breakthroughs of recent decades . . . TEE started as a means of training pastors while in the ministry. It has rapidly spread round the world and diversified into distance learning courses at all levels from basic to degree-earning."

CLTC TEE has for the most part been used as general Christian education rather than leadership training. Many of our new courses however are more specifically aimed at leadership. The point I would like to emphasize from Operation World and even from our own experience is that TEE is flexible in being used to meet different training needs of different situations.

In the last three years, the Bible College of New Zealand (BCNZ) has been very instrumental in establishing TEE programs in two sister South Pacific Association of Bible Colleges (SPABC) Bible colleges in Australia, Bible College of Victoria (BCV), and Bible College of Queensland (BCQ). BCNZ use a combination of TAFTEE, SEAN, and CLTC TEE materials and all these have gone across to BCV and BCQ. Establishing TEE programs in interdenominational evangelical institutions such as these would be a good approach for the Islands if there were other such interdenominational evangelical Colleges besides CLTC.

Chile

I'm sure there are hundreds of experiences and testimonies concerning the vitality of TEE in ministry today. I count it a privilege and joy to share a recent letter from Terrick J. Barrett, International Director of SEAN in Chile. We remember that in 1971, he was serving as a missionary in Tucaman, Argentina. He also remained committed to helping the Mapuche Indians in Chile. It was he and an excellent team that developed the series on the life of Christ now famous as the "Compendium of Pastoral Theology." He writes:

As regards to your question: Is SEAN alive and well? I rejoice in the Lord to be able to give an absolute YES!!

In brief SEAN courses are currently used in about 110 countries and in 77 languages (at our last count).

It would be difficult to give details as to the varied use our courses get, so I would like to illustrate by giving just one example.

I have just returned from Argentina, where we celebrated the 20th anniversary of FLET (International Faculty of Theological Study). This TEE program is extended throughout Argentina and over the past twenty years has touched 36,000 students, of which 6,000 have completed the different Certificates and Diplomas. But that is just statistics, what has happened at a church level?

Well, for starts, a robed choir led the ceremony from a church of over 600 members, all whose pastors and leaders were trained using SEAN Courses in FLET. Fourteen years ago that same church had about eighty members, and the pastor attributes the growth, to the "ministry of the Saints training" as espoused by Sean TEE. Many other churches were also represented; all of which had the same story to tell.

Not only that, theologians and leaders of Residential Seminaries were also present at the celebration. For now TEE is not an 'either/or' cheap second-rate alternative to theological study. It is vital at local church level. So now pastors and ministers lay and ordained alike, are trained on the job, and those who wish to extend their studies all the way up to degree level. Gone are the days, when the raw young student went directly to a residential seminary. These institutions are now being fed with students proven first on the battlefront.

But the Argentina story doesn't end there. Sean is repeatedly getting letters from all over the world, where FLET trained missionaries are requesting authorization to translate our courses into the languages where they are now ministering. So the pattern is repeating itself in such places as Albania, CIS, Ukraine, Mozambique, Italy, Spain, Morocco, and many others.

FLET is also extended to many other countries in Latin America, and I could tell you many similar stories from their experience. So, quite definitively, Sean TEE has come of age, and is being used by God for the extension of His Kingdom.

To Him and Him alone be all honor and glory.

In closing, we cite Covell's perspective comment:
The church must grow qualitatively in a biblical knowledge, in Christian piety, and in many forms of dedicated service. Pastors long for renewed learning opportunities. If they must leave their sphere of ministry and go away to school, both quantitative and qualitative growth will suffer! How far superior to train them where they are as they continue to serve Christ. The extension seminary and church growth? In a nutshell, decentralized theological education enables us to prepare more and better leaders on a variety of levels and from a variety of homogeneous cultural units. These men will take places of innovative leadership within rapidly multiplying new churches and spearhead evangelistic outreach into whitened harvest fields.[1]

---

[1] Covell, 132.

APPENDICES

1. Some Generally Accepted Principles of Learning
2. Suggestions for the Use of Questions
3. Open Education
4. Kinds of Frames to Use in Writing PI Materials
5. Leaders: Example of Target Group Identification
6. Earl V. Pullias, *Goals for Teachers*
7. Bibliographies
8. Ralph D. Winter, *The Largest Stumbling Block to Leadership Development in the Global Church*
9. Ralph D. Winter, *Thoughts about Jim Emery (and TEE): On the Occasion of His Funeral, Friday, August 27, 1999*

SOME GENERALLY ACCEPTED PRINCIPLES OF LEARNING

Schools of psychological thought are so numerous and so varied in their viewpoints about learning that a real service has been rendered by scholars who have tried to reconcile the differing viewpoints. Two of these scholars are Ernest R. Hilgard and Goodwin Watson. On the following pages, quotations and paraphrases of some of Hilgard's and Watson's statements are presented. The statements chosen have special interest for teachers and other curriculum workers.

A motivated learner acquires what he learns more readily than one who is not motivated. The relevant motives include both general and specific ones, for example, desire to learn, need for achievement (general), desire for a reward or for avoidance of a threatened punishment (specific).

Motivation that is too intense (especially pain, fear, and anxiety) may be accompanied by distracting emotional states so that excessive motivation may be less effective than moderate motivation for learning some kinds of tasks, particularly those involving difficult discriminations.

Learning under the control of reward is usually preferable to learning under the control of punishment. Correspondingly, learning motivated by success is preferable to learning motivated by failure. Even though the theoretical issue is still unresolved, the practical outcome must take into account the social by-products, which tend to be more favorable under reward than under punishment.

Learning under intrinsic motivation is preferable to learning under extrinsic motivation.

Tolerance of failure is best taught through providing a backlog of success.

Individuals need practice in setting goals for themselves: goals which are neither so low and limited as to elicit little effort nor so high and difficult as to foreordain failure. Realistic goal setting leads to more satisfactory improvement than does unrealistic goal setting.

The personal history of the individual—for example, his record of reaction to authority—may hamper or enhance his ability to learn from a given teacher.

Active participation by learners is preferable to passive reception of the content to be learned.

Meaningful materials are learned more readily than nonsense materials, meaningful tasks more readily than tasks not understood by the learner.

There is no substitute for repetitive practice in the overlearning of skills or in the memorization of unrelated facts which must be automatized.

Information about the nature of a good performance, knowledge of one's mistakes, and
knowledge of successful results assist the
learner.

Transfer to new tasks will occur more smoothly
if, in learning, the learner can discover relationships for himself and has experience in
applying principles of relationship within a
variety of tasks.

Spaced or distributed recalls are advantageous in
fixing material that is to be retained a long time.

Learners progress in any area of learning only as
far as they need to in order to achieve their
purpose. Often they do only well enough to "get
by"; with increased motivation they improve.

The most effective effort is put forth by children
when they attempt tasks which fall in the "range
of challenge"—not too easy and not too
hard—where success seems quite possible but
not certain.

Learners engage in an activity most willingly if
they have helped select and plan the activity.

When learners are grouped by ability according
to any one criterion such as age, I.Q., or reading
ability, they vary over a range of several grades
according to other criteria.

Learners think when they encounter obstacles or challenges to action that interest them. In thinking, they design and test plausible ways of overcoming the obstacles or challenges.

When pupils learn concepts, they need to have the concepts presented in varied and specific situation. Then they should try the concepts in situations different from those in which they were originally learned.

Pupils learn a great deal from each other. When they have been together a long time, they learn from each other more rapidly than they do from peers who are strange to them.

The problem of "isolates" appears in every school. Isolates are those children who are generally not chosen by their classmates and who are also likely to be unpopular with teachers.

No school subject is strikingly superior to any other subject for strengthening one's mental powers.

Pupils remember new subject matter that conforms with their previous attitudes better than they remember new subject matter that opposes their previous attitudes.

Learning is aided by formulating and asking questions that stimulate thinking and imagination.

SUGGESTIONS FOR THE USE OF QUESTIONS

1. Types of Questions:
   a. Factual: seek information
   b. Thought-provoking: usually "why" or "how" questions
   c. Rhetorical: no answer intended
   d. Contact: simple question used to establish contact with new student
2. Helps in the use of questions:
   a. Plan the questions that you will use in your lessons. Also, try to anticipate questions which the pupils will raise.
   b. Use "yes" and "no" questions sparingly. They do not stimulate thought. If the pupil does not know the answer, he is tempted to guess.
   c. Ask questions that are simple, direct, and clear. Long or difficult questions are confusing to the pupil. If he is confused about the question, restate it in another way. However, if the pupil was not paying attention, do not repeat it.
   d. Ask the question and then direct it to the individual. This involves the whole class in the process.
   e. At the beginning of the class let the pupils know that you will expect information and opinion from them. This will produce an alert, participating class.
   f. Endeavor to develop the skill of answering a question with a question. This develops a questioning mind on the part of the student.
   g. Never ridicule any question, no matter how silly it may appear to you.
   h. If you ask a question, give ample opportunity for someone to answer. Do not be afraid of silence. Students may be thinking.

i. Ask questions promiscuously. Pupils tend to be more alert when they don't know if they will be called upon.

j. Use questions to gain, regain, and maintain interest.

k. Encourage and stimulate questions from the pupil. His questions often reveal his needs.

OPEN EDUCATION

Open education is an approach to education that is open to change, to new ideas, to curriculum, to scheduling, between teacher and pupil and between pupil and pupil, and open to children's participation in significant decision-making in the classroom.

Open education is characterized by a classroom environment in which there is a minimum of teaching in the class as a whole, in which provision is made for children to pursue individual interests and to direct many aspects of their own learning.

The following fifteen characteristics constitutes the basic model of an open classroom; every open classroom will reflect them in varying degrees.

1. A minimum of lessons for the whole class; most instruction geared to small groups or individuals.
2. A variety of activities progressing simultaneously.
3. Flexible scheduling, so that children can engage in different activities for varying periods of time.
4. An environment rich in materials, both commercial and homemade.
5. Freedom for children to move about, converse, work together, and ask help from one another.
6. Opportunities for children to make decisions about their work and to develop responsibility for setting and meeting their educational goals.
7. Lack of rigid, prescribed curriculum and provision for children to investigate matters of concern to them.
8. Some integration of the curriculum, eliminating isolated teaching of each subject.

9. Emphasis on experimentation and involvement with materials.
10. Flexible learning groups formed around interests, as well as academic needs, and organized by both pupils and teachers.
11. An atmosphere of trust, acceptance of children, and respect for their diversity.
12. Attention to individual intellectual, emotional, physical, and social needs.
13. Creative activities valued as part of the curriculum.
14. A minimum of grading and marking.
15. Honest and open relationship between teacher and pupil and between pupil and pupil; teacher avoidance of exploiting authority.

The Teacher's Guide to Open Education, Lillian Stephens.

KINDS OF FRAMES TO USE IN WRITING PI MATERIALS

Once we have the daily objective clearly stated, we must then handle this bit of information from an angle so it becomes fixed in the student's mind. Though we are doing linear (straight line) programming, in a sense we are circling around the objective. We must come back to the desired response again and again, each time giving less help, until the student can perform the objective in the terminal frame without any help at all.

The kinds of frames we list here are not official. You will not find them in any book. But they are tools which we have found useful and we have just given them names for convenience. They do not all have to be used in each day's program. Also, you are not limited to using each kind only once in a day. Use any combination that fits your purpose, but try to have a variety. In some cases, one from will fulfill two or more functions.

Avoid copy frames in which you tell the student something and then just ask him to tell it back to you. Your questions should cause the student to turn the information around in his head and use it before answering.

1. *Introduction frame.* State what it is you are going to teach the student in this lesson. Give the exact response you want at the end. This is rather like stating your objective to the student. This will be the nearest to a copy frame which you may be able to use. This is sometimes called a set frame. (Example *in Bringing People to Jesus*, by Fred Holland, 50-55).

2. *Value frame.* To help the student see why he should achieve this objective. This would help approach behavior. (Page 139, Frame 3).
3. *Proof frame.* Show how the Bible teaches this thing. Give him a verse or verses from the Bible and ask him to pick out the thing which applies to your objective. (Page 42, Frame 6).
4. *Convincing frame.* Give something which the student has likely seen in his own life. Use this to convince him that the objective is true. (Page 121, Frame 3).
5. *Building-block frame.* Give part of the objective and ask the student to give you another part. This should be done for each part of the objective so there should be several of these in every day's lesson. (Page 136, Frame 9).
6. *Example frame.* Present the student with an example of the definition or rule you are asking him to learn and ask him to identify it. This can be an example from the Bible or from life in general. (Page 189, Frame 12).
7. *Practice frames.* If you are teaching a definition, give the student the definition and ask him to give the term. (Page 10, Frame 7). Or give the student the term and ask him to give the definition. (Page 10, Frames 6 and 8). If you are teaching a rule, ask the student to identify an example or non-example of it. (Page 75, Frames 6 and 7; Page 85, Frame 11).
8. *Discrimination frame.* Ask the student to identify examples of your rule or definition from among many choices. (Page 198, Frame 13).
9. *Experience frame.* After describing a certain situation or problem, ask the student whether this has ever happened to him. This is good in some

cases to get the student to relate the lesson to himself, but should not be overdone.

10. *Application frame.* After presenting a teaching, ask the student to give an answer that shows how he can use this in his own life. (Frame 6). Or ask the student to write several lines about his reaction to the present objective or objectives. This is useful in testing affective objectives, except that they may not be wholly voluntary. (Frame 6).

11. *Review or revision frame.* Whenever you can, slip in a question which makes the student use some of the objective which he has already learned in the course. (In *Bring People to Jesus*, we reviewed the previous day's objective at the beginning of each new lesson, and gave three days of review questions during the course which included review questions in regular lessons where possible. (Page 196, Frame 4).

12. *Clarification frame.* When the meaning of the objective may not be fully clear, a frame can be put in to clear this up. The student's response in this case will be an interim objective, and he will not be expected to give this answer in the end. (Page 136, Frame 8).

13. *Cultural frame.* To explain how the given objective applies particularly in Africa. This is often accomplished by an example frame, but culture needs to be kept in mind. (Page 34, Frame 5; Page 48, Frame 10). The cultural application here is not direct, but it is present. Though some of the wrong motives are found everywhere, the idea of evangelism as a civilized or honor-demanding job may be more common in Africa. (Page 79, Frame 7 implies that in parts of rural Africa, at least, visiting

back and forth is very desirable, therefore, it is a good means of evangelism.)

14. *Memorization frame.* Sometimes you will want your students to memorize Scripture verses. Don't try to program this, just tell him to stop and do it before he goes on. Our level of student cannot be expected to memorize more than one verse per week.

15. *Self-examination frame.* Sometimes it is good to tell the student to stop, examine himself in relation to the objective and pray about it. There is no written response to this and it should not be overdone. (Page 50, Frame 2).

16. *Terminal or criterion frame.* There is no new information given in this frame. The student is simply asked to perform the objective. There should be one of these at the end of every day's lesson. (Page 86, Frame 14; Page 15, 13).

LEADERS: EXAMPLE OF TARGET GROUP IDENTIFICATION

The Target Group for this study is the group of leaders (elders, pastors) in the local churches (congregations, assemblies) in Latin American countries and Spain. Though there are deep-seated syncretistic elements in each of these cultures that affect the heart (or gut) level attitudes and reactions of these people, the world-view is that which is primarily received from a Latin, Catholic society. The world-view of these leaders has changed through their knowledge of Jesus Christ as Savior and Lord. This does not mean that their world-view, their cosmology is Western at its core. They all have been influenced by Western technology to varying degrees according to the individual. If the person lives in a rural society, he will be less influenced by technology but may still have some gut level attitudes toward animistic practices or superstitions prominent in the region. Certainly the Latin culture will influence him substantially: 1. The strong family unit, 2. The social structure, including attitudes of group rather than self-centered individualism. Because they are evangelical Christian a lot of their theological positions have been changed especially regarding the doctoral positions of the Catholic church.

As to education, we are writing primarily for those of basic schooling, that is, for those with a primary educational level. We trust also that those with less than four years of schooling and those with more than sixth grade education will find the study valuable. The abilities, then, of those who are in the target group would necessarily be that of reading and writing, basic primary school vocabulary, some ability for logical thinking, and a great desire for growing in the Lord and the knowledge and practice of His Word. The target group would be those who are already active in their local congregations but need help in developing leadership qualities as well as to "where they are going" as church leaders.

GOALS FOR TEACHERS
by EARL V. PULLIAS

The most nearly universal traits of great teachers, in my judgement, are:

1. Integrity or authenticity: a freedom from phoniness or pretense, an approach to genuineness and utter sincerity.
2. Enthusiasm or zest: an ardent belief in the significance of what one is doing and the energy to put life into it.
3. Directness or nearness to reality: a trait manifested in an almost childlike relation to things and people, an elemental quality of immediacy that escapes the deadening, heavy hand of pedantry and over-abstraction.
4. Perspective or length and breadth of view: manifested frequently in a sense of humor, patience, freedom from the scourge of perfectionism.
5. Freedom of mind, especially freedom of imagination: a trait that encourages ideas to flow freely, an eagerness to consider many alternatives.
6. Breadth of interest or sensitivity to a wide spectrum of life: manifested in wide reading and varied concerns.
7. An abiding concern for the individual learner: an ability to feel and communicate the notion that the individual learner is significant, that he has potential of great worth and that it can be realized.

More fundamental than any list of attributes or traits (which at best can only be illustrative) is the principle that the effective teacher must be alive and growing. This growth must be taking place in two great dimensions of personality and character: knowledge and being.

In *Toward Excellence in College Training*, 44-45.

BIBLIOGRAPHY

Allen, Roland. *Missionary Methods*. City World Dominion Press. 1960.

Amirtham, Samuel. "New Styles in Theological Education." *Evangelical Review of Theology*, April, 1979.

Bakulumpagi-Kabazzii, Richard. "Contextualizing Theological Programmes." *Education Newsletter*, No. 1, 1974. Geneva: World Council of Churches.

Bakulumpagi-Kabazzii, Richard. "Focal Points of Authentic Renewal." *Education Newsletter*, No. 4, December, 1972.Geneva: World Council of Churches.

Barrett, Tony. *Issues in Latin America*. Evangelical Missions Quarterly. 1986.

Batlle, Agustin and Rosario. "Theological Community of Chile: Extension Training for Indigenous Church Leaders," *Ministerial Formation*, January, 1982.

Bergquist, James A. "Village Ministries and TEE in India: A Case of Unfulfilled Potential?" *Extension Seminary*, No. 2, 1974.

Briggs, Leslie J. *Instructional Design*. Englewood Cliffs: Educational Theology Publications. 1977.

Bruce, A. B. *The Training of the Twelve*. Edinburgh: T. and T. Clark. 1908.

Coleman, Robert E. *The Master Plan of Evangelism.* New York: Revell. 1964.

Conn, Harvie M. "Theological Education and the Search for Excellence." *Westminster Theological Journal,* Spring, 1979.

Coombs, Philip. *New Paths to Learning for Rural Children and Youth.*

Covell, Ralph R. and Peter C. Wagner. *An Extension Seminary Primer.* South Pasadena: William Carey Library, 1971.

Crider, Donald William. "The Development and Rationale of Theological Education by Extension of the Free Methodist Church in South Africa with a Programmed Pastoral Theology Text for Africa." Th.M. Thesis, School of World Mission, Fuller Theological Seminary. 1980.

Elliston, Edgar J. *Developing Leaders at a Distance: Contextualizing Leadership Development.* Fuller Theological Seminary, 1997.

Elliston, Edgar J. *Theological Education by Extension,* ML540 Syllabus, Pasadena: Fuller Theological Seminary. 1986.

Emery, James H. "The Traditional and the Extension Seminary: Conflict or Cooperation—Friends or Enemies?" *Theological Education by Extension.* Ralph D. Winter, Ed. 219.

Enns, Arno. *Man Milieu and Mission in Argentina.* Grand Rapids: Eerdmans. 1980.

Espich, James and Bill Williams. *Developing Programmed Instructional Materials*. Palo Alto: Fearon Publishers. 1967.

Gerber, Vergil, ed. *Discipling Through Theological Education by Extension*. Chicago: Moody Press. 1980.

Graybill, John B. "School" in the *Zondervan Pictorial Bible Dictionary*. Merrill C. Tenny, ed. Grand Rapids: Zondervan Publishing House. 1963.

Hay, Alexander R. *The New Testament Order for Church and Missionary*. Buenos Aires: New Testament Missionary Union. 1947.

Helder, Dom. "National Study Consultation on Theological Training of the Whole Church and New Patterns of Training," *Extension Seminary*, No. 2, 1975.

Hill, D. Leslie. *Designing a Theological Education by Extension Program: A Philippine Case Study*. Pasadena: William Carey Library. 1974.

Holland, Fred. *Teaching Through TEE: Help for Leaders in Theological Education by Extension in Africa*. Kisumu: Evangel Press. 1975.

Holland, Fred. "Text-Africa Programming for Ministry Through Theological Education by Extension." *Ministerial Formation*, January, 1982.

Hulbert, Terry C. "The Quest for Renewal in Theological Education." *East Africa Journal of Evangelical Theology*, No. 1, 1988.

Kaller, Donald W. "TEE: Brazil's Success Story." *Christianity Today*, February 13, 1976. 13-14.

Kinsler, Ross. *The Extension Movement in Theological Education*. Pasadena: William Carey Library, 1977.

Kinsler, Ross. *Ministry by the People, Theological Education by Extension*. Mary Knoll: Orbis Books. 1983.

Kinsler, Ross and James Emery. *Opting for Change*. William Carey Library. 1992.

Kornfield, William J. "The Challenge to Make Extension Education Culturally Relevant." *Evangelical Missions Quarterly*, January, 1976. 13-22.

Markel, Susan M. *Good Frames and Bad*. New York: John Wiley. 1969.

McGavran, Donald A. *How Churches Grow*. London: World Dominion Press. 1959.

McKinney, Lois. "Leadership, Key to Church Growth. " *Discipling through TEE*. Gerber.

McKinney, Lois. "Training for Our Generation." Paper presented at the EFMA/IFMA Study Conference, Kansas City, Missouri, September, 1981.

McKinney, Lois. *Writing for Theological Education by Extension.* Pasadena: William Carey Library. 1975.

Mulholland, Kenneth B. *Adventures in Training the Ministry: A Honduran Case Study in Theological Education by Extension.* Philadelphia: Presbyterian and Reformed Publishing Company. 1976.

Padilla, Rene. "Hermeneutics and Culture—A Theological Perspective." *Gospel and Culture.* Scott and Coote. 1979.

Padilla, C. Rene. "The Interpreted Word: Reflections on Contextual Hermeneutics." *Themelios,* September, 1981.

Patterson, George. *Obedience-Oriented Education.* Portland, n.p. 1976.

Patterson, George and Richard Scoggins. *Multiplication Guide.* Pasadena: William Carey Library. 1994.

Pipe, Peter. *Practical Programming.* Huntington: Robert E. Kreiger Publishing Company. 1977.

Plueddeman, J. E. "Toward a Theology of Theological Education." Evangelical Theological Education Today: Agenda for Renewal, Paul Bowers (ed.). Nairobi: Evangel Publishing House. 1982.

Popham, W. James and Eva I. Baker. *Establishing Instructional Goals*. Englewood Cliffs: Prentice-Hall, Inc. 1970.

Porter, H. Boone. "The Tent Maker and Theological Education." *Seminario de Extension*, No. 2, Apartado 3, 1973. San Felipe, Reu., Guatemala.

Read, William R., Victor M. Monterroso, and Harmon A. Johnson. *Latin American Church Growth*. Grand Rapids: Eerdmans. 1969.

Rowen, Samuel. "Teeing Off With TEE." *Christianity Today*, April 27, 1972.

Sauer, James B. "TEE in Zaire—Mission or Movement?" *Evangelical Review of Theology*, October, 1978.

Savage, Peter. "A Bold Move for More Realistic Theological Training." *Evangelical Mission Quarterly*, Winter, 1969.

Sprunger, Fritz. *TEE in Japan*. Pasadena: William Carey Library. 1981.

Taber, Charles R. "Theological Education in Africa with Stress on Theological Education by Extension." *African Theological Journal*, Vol. 8, No. 1.

Taber, Charles S. "The Limits of Indigenization in Theology." *Missiology*, 1978.

Ward, Margaret and Ted. *Programmed Instruction for Theological Education*. Committee to Assist Missionary Education Overseas (CAMEO). 1970.

Ward, Ted. "Nonformal Education: What is it?" *Handbook of the Nonformal Education Institute.*

Ward, Ted. "Types of TEE" *The Evangelical Missions Quarterly*, April, 1979. 74-85.

Ward, Ted and Samuel Rowen. "The Significance of the Extension Seminary." *Evangelical Mission Quarterly*, Fall, 1972.

Weld, Wayne C. "The Extension Seminary." *Quarterly Bulletin*, November 2, 1977.

Weld, Wayne C. *The World Directory of Theological Education by Extension.* Pasadena: William Carey Library. 1973.

Winter, Ralph D. *Theological Education by Extension.* Pasadena: William Carey Library. 1973.

Youngblood, Robert L., ed. *A Reader in Theological Education.* Drubergen: World Evangelical Fellowship, 1983.

The following very helpful bibliography is supplied by Edgar J. Elliston.

Albrecht, Robert and Gary Bardsley
    1994   "Strategic Planning and Academic Planning for Distance Education," In Barry Willis (Ed.) *Distance Education Strategies and Tools.* Englewood Cliffs, NJ: Educational Technology Publications. pp. 67-86.

Aleshire, Daniel O.
    1988   *Faith Care: Ministering to All God's People Through the Ages of Life.* Philadelphia: Westminster Press.

Barker, Joel
    1992   *Future Edge.*

Blanch, Gregory
    1994   "Don't All Faculty Want Their Own TV Show? Barriers to Faculty Participation in Distance Education," *Deosnews.* DEOS—The Distance Education Online Symposium Published in collaboration with the American Journal of Distance Education and the American Center for the Study of Distance Education, The Pennsylvania State University. 4:1.

Brace, Sylvia Bedwell and Gina Roberts
1997 "When Payup Becomes Payback: A University's Return on Instructional Technology Investment," Syllabus '97 Conference. Sonoma State University, Rohnert Park, CA. July 28-31.

Brown, F. Barry and Yvonne Brown
1994 "Distance Education Around the World," In Barry Willis (Ed.) *Distance Education Strategies and Tools*. Englewood Cliffs, NJ: Educational Technology Publications. pp. 3-40.

Dede, Chris
1993 "Trends and Forecasts in Distance Education," *Educom Review*. November/December 28:6. EDUCOM, 1112 16th St., N.W., Suite 600, Washington, DC 20036; 202 872-4200; via e-mail: EDUCOM@BITNIC.EDUCOM.EDU.

Foa, J. Lin
1993 "Technology and Change: Composing a Four Part Harmony," EDUCOM Review, 28:2 (March/April)

Eastmond, Nick
1994 "Assessing Needs, Developing Instruction, and Evaluating Results in Distance Education," In Barry Willis (Ed.) *Distance Education Strategies and Tools*. Englewood Cliffs, NJ: Educational Technology Publications. pp. 87-108.

Elliston, Edgar J. and J. Timothy Kauffman
1993   *Developing Leaders for Urban Ministry*. New York: Peter Lang Publishers.

Freeman, Robert
1996   "Design and Development of a Strategic Planning Process for the Continuing and Extended Education Division of Fuller Theological Seminary." Ed.D. dissertation, Nova Southwestern University.

Friere, Paulo
1970   *Pedagogy of the Oppressed*. New York: The Seabury Press.

Frishberg, Nancy
1997   "Technology Coupon Cutting: Faculty Support on a Shoestring," Syllabus '97 Conference. Sonoma State University, Rohnert Park, CA. July 28-31.

Fuller Theological Seminary
1996   "Communicorp Report."

Goulet, Daniel and Randall P. Peelen
1997   "It Takes More than Two to Tango: A "Team Building" Model for Educational Technology," Syllabus '97 Conference. Sonoma State University, Rohnert Park, CA. July 28-31.

Grove, Andrew S.
1995 *Only the Paranoid Survive.* New York: Doubleday.

Guang, Alberto
1990 Personal Interview.

Hammett, Paula
1997 "Information Literacy and the Evaluation of Web-based Resources," Syllabus '97 Conference. Sonoma State University, Rohnert Park, CA. July 28-31.

Harry, K. J. and D. Keegan (Eds.)
1993 *Distance Education: New Perspectives.* London: Routledge.

Holmberg, B.
1986 *Growth and Structure of Distance Education.* London: Croom Helm.

1993 "Key Issues in Distance Education: An Academic Viewpoint," In Harry, K. J. and Keegan, D. (Eds.). *Distance Education: New Perspectives.* London: Routledge. pp. 330-341.

Jewett, Frank
1997 "Case Study Manual Evaluating the Benefits and Costs of Mediated Instruction and Distributed Learning," Syllabus '97 Conference. Sonoma State University, Rohnert Park, CA. July 28-31.

Kearsley, Greg and William Lynch (Eds.)
1994 *Educational Technology Leadership Perspectives*. Englewood Cliffs, NJ: Educational Technology Publications.

Keegan, D.
1990 "A Theory of Distance Education," In Michael G. Moore (Ed.), *Contemporary Issues in American Distance Education*. Oxford, UK: Pergamon Press. pp. 327-332.

Kemp, Stephen
1996 "A Silent Success: Church-Based Seminary Extension Education," *Access Newsletter*. December 10:1:1-3.

Kendall, Janet Ross and Muriel Oaks
1992 "Evaluation of Perceived Teaching Effectiveness: Course Delivery Via Interactive Video Technology Versus Traditional Classroom Methods," *Deosnews*. DEOS—The Distance Education Online Symposium Published in collaboration with the American Journal of Distance Education and the American Center for the Study of Distance Education, The Pennsylvania State University. 2:5.

Kinsler, F. Ross
1985 *Ministry by the People*. New York: Orbis.

Knowles, Malcolm
1990   *The Adult Learner A Neglected Species*. (Fourth Edition). Houston: Gulf Publishing Company.

Lauzon, Allan C. and George A. B. Moore
1989   "A Fourth Generation Distance Education System: Integrating Computer Assisted Learning and Computer Conferencing" *Journal of Distance Education*, 3:1:38-49.

McGavran, Donald A.
1969   "Five Kinds of Leaders." A lecture delivered at Columbia Bible College.

McGill, Mollie A. and Sally M. Johnstone
1994   "Distance Education: An Opportunity for Cooperation and Resource Sharing," In Barry Willis (Ed.) *Distance Education Strategies and Tools*. Englewood Cliffs, NJ: Educational Technology Publications. pp. 258-264.

Miller, Gary E.
1992   "Long-Term Trends in Distance Education," *Deosnews*. DEOS—The Distance Education Online Symposium Published in collaboration with the American Journal of Distance Education and the American Center for the Study of Distance Education, The Pennsylvania State University. 2:23.

Moore, Michael G. (Ed.)
1990   *Contemporary Issues in American Distance Education.* Oxford, UK: Pergamon Press, pp. 327-332.

1990   "Recent Contributions to the Theory of Distance Education," *Open Learning.* 5:3:10-15.

1991   "Theory of Distance Education." Paper presented at The Second American Symposium on Research in Distance Education, May 22-24, The Pennsylvania State University, University Park, PA.

Murphy, K.
1988   "Introducing Teleconferencing to Turkey—Partnerships That Work!" *The Australian Journal of Educational Technology*, 5:1:14-22.

Oxley, Simon
1997   "The Local Congregation as a Learning Community," *Education Newsletter.* Program Unit II, Churches in Mission: Health, Education, Witness. 1:1.

Patterson, Elizabeth
1996   "The Questions of Distance Education," *Theological Education.* 33:1:59-74.

Paulsen, Morten Flate
    1993   "The Hexagon of Cooperative Freedom: A
            Distance Education Theory Attuned to
            Computer Conferencing," *Deosnews*. DEOS—
            The Distance Education Online Symposium
            Published in collaboration with the American
            Journal of Distance Education and the American
            Center for the Study of Distance Education, The
            Pennsylvania State University. 2:23.

Peters, O.
    1993   "Understanding Distance Education," In K. J.
            Harry and D. Keegan (Eds.). *Distance
            Education: New Perspectives*. London:
            Routledge. pp. 10-18.

Peterson, Mark L.
    1997   "Providing Effective Technical Support in a
            Distance Learning Environment," Syllabus '97
            Conference. Sonoma State University, Rohnert
            Park, CA. July 28-31.

Pittman, Von V.
    1990   "Correspondence Study in the American
            University: A Historiographic Perspective." In
            Michael G. Moore, *Contemporary Issues in
            American Distance Education*. Oxford: Pergamon
            Press, pp. 67-80.

Saba, F.

1990 "Integrated Telecommunication System and Instructional Transaction." In M. G. Moore (Ed.), *Contemporary Issues in American Distance Education*. Oxford, UK: Pergamon Press. pp. 344-352.

1994 "Educational Radio and Television of Iran: A Retrospective, 1973-1978. *Educational Technology Research and Development*, 42:2:73-84.

1994b "From Development Communication to Systems Thinking: A Post-Modern Analysis of Distance Education in the International Arena. In Conference Proceedings of the International Distance Education Conference, June 1994, University Park, PA.

Saba, F., and R.L. Shearer

1994 "Verifying Key Theoretical Concepts in a Dynamic Model of Distance Education." *The American Journal of Distance Education*, 8:1:36-59.

Saba, F. and D. Twitchell

1988 "Research in Distance Education: A System Modeling Approach," *The American Journal of Distance Education*. 2:1:9-24.

1988/89 "Integrated Services Digital Networks: How It Can Be Used for Distance Education," *Journal of Educational Technology Systems.* 17:1:15-25.

Schosser, Charles A. and Mary L. Anderson
1994   *Distance Education: Review of the Literature.* Ames: IA: Iowa State University.

Shale, D.
1990   "Toward a Reconceptualization of Distance Education. In Michael G. Moore (Ed.), *Contemporary Issues in American Distance Education.* Oxford, UK: Pergamon Press. pp. 333-343.

Shuster, Marguerite
1997   Personal interview.

Skinner, Bob
1997   "Instructional Computing at SMU," Syllabus '97 Conference. Sonoma State University, Rohnert Park, CA. July 28-31.

Threlkeld, Robert and Karen Brzoska
1994   "Research in Distance Education," In Barry Willis (Ed.) *Distance Education Strategies and Tools.* Englewood Cliffs, NJ: Educational Technology Publications. pp. 41-66.

Venditti, Nicolas
1997   Personal interview.

Verduin, John R., Jr. and Thomas A. Clark
1991 *Distance Education: The Foundations of Effective Practice.* San Francisco: Jossey-Bass Publishers.

Vines, Diane
1997 "Larger Scale Distance Learning Initiatives," Syllabus '97 Conference. Sonoma State University, Rohnert Park, CA. July 28-31.

Walls, Francine and Jim Shuman
1997 "Learning How To Learn," Syllabus '97 Conference. Sonoma State University, Rohnert Park, CA. July 28-31.

Ward, Ted W.
1973 "Split Rail Fence Analogy" *Evangelical Missions Quarterly.*

1994 "Integrity of Method and Objective," *Access Newsletter.* November, 8:2:1,4-5.

1996 "Servants, Leaders, and Tyrants," In Duane Elmer and Lois McKinney (Eds.), *With an Eye on the Future Development and Mission in the 21st Century.* Monrovia: MARC. pp. 27-32.

Willis, Barry
1993 *Distance Education: A Practical Guide.* Englewood Cliffs, NJ: Educational Technology Publications.

1994   "Enhancing Faculty Effectiveness in Distance Education," In Barry Willis (Ed.) *Distance Education Strategies and Tools*. Englewood Cliffs, NJ: Educational Technology Publications. pp. 277-290.

Willis, Barry (Ed.)

1994   *Distance Education Strategies and Tools*. Englewood Cliffs, NJ: Educational Technology Publications.

THE LARGEST STUMBLING BLOCK TO LEADERSHIP DEVELOPMENT IN THE GLOBAL CHURCH*
by RALPH D. WINTER

I'm a little embarrassed by this topic. It may sound pompous. There are, of course, other problems besides the one to which I refer. However, I will say that from my point of view I am definitely talking about the major stumbling block in leadership development in the global church.

I'm not going to let you wonder until the very end just what I think that stumbling block is. I refer very simply to the far-reaching practice of selecting the wrong people for training. This is, I believe, the largest stumbling block in leadership development in the global church.

First of all, why would we—and I include myself as part of the theological education movement—why would we select the wrong people for training? Why, all over the world, would we put enormous sums of money and manpower into *training the wrong people?*

You can see why this simple statement of the problem requires further comment. Just to state it seems baldly and hopelessly erroneous. How could it possibly be true?

Note carefully that, first of all, if you spend your energies training the wrong people, you bypass the right people. You in effect suppress the training of the right people if you are using up your time and facilities and resources training

---

*
On January 15, 1998, the annual conference of the Association of Christian Continuing Education Schools and Seminaries known as ACCESS met on the campus of the U.S. Center for World Mission. The above is based on transcripts of the opening address delivered by Ralph D. Winter.

the wrong people. All over the world, especially in the United States, but also wherever the "long hand" of the Western church reaches, the more gifted leaders of the Christian movement are being sidetracked and are *not being recruited* into ministry in much of the world church.

Let's go to Africa. In Africa the majority of those who follow Christ, who seek the living God, and for whom the Bible is the most prominent feature of their movement are not the people whom we would normally call Christians. They are part of a very wide spectrum of movements earlier called the *African Independent Churches*, and then the *African Indigenous Churches*, and now more recently I hear it is the *African Initiated Churches* (AIC). People are struggling to gain respectable terminology for a movement that has long been considered quite unrespectable. But David Barrett claims there are more than 50 million Africans in this movement!

When the great GCOWE meeting took place in Pretoria, South Africa in July, 1997, with more countries and ethnic groups represented than at any earlier Christian meeting in human history, this entire, massive African category wasn't represented. Many of its leaders are illiterate. Illiterate people aren't eager to go to "respectable" Christian meetings. These people are so far off the beaten track that, while they are referred to as "churches," most of them don't even employ the word "Christian." Most of our mission organizations have nothing to do with this dimension of the Christian movement. I wish it were not true.

Nevertheless, on the first evening of that meeting in Pretoria, they presented a 96-year-old man who looked like he was in pretty good shape. Seventy years earlier he had gone out as a young missionary to Africa from the Assemblies of God. I am not sure how he got in with the AIC movement. In his work he was so earnest that he didn't even insist that these people form Assemblies of God churches. To make a long story short, the board back home said, "We're not going to support a missionary who isn't going to produce Assemblies of God churches. What in the world do you think you are working for? The Kingdom?" (That is not an exact quote!) You know, that kind of thing.

After a few years Dr. McGavran heard about this and prevailed on the people in Springfield to take him back in. And he was back in for a while, and then I guess he was out again. Anyway, here he is on the platform being honored after seventy years of ministry in Africa, and he's practically the only foreign missionary who has taken seriously what is now a movement of 50 million people!

Notice that there isn't anything we have ever said in an ACCESS meeting that would have anything useful to say to this movement. Most of our education employs the printed page, doesn't it? These people can't read. What do you do about that? There are ways to deal with that, but we are not really very high on that sort of thing.

Let's go to Latin America, to Brazil. Again, seven out of eight new churches—and there are about ten or fifteen new ones a week, someone said fifty, who knows?—almost all of them are Pentecostal. They don't have seminaries. They don't believe in seminaries. That isn't quite true: they now finally have a seminary in the United States and are inheriting all the problems go along with it. In any event, Latin America is a very rapidly growing sphere of world Christianity, but some feel it is not growing "properly," "respectably," "normally." It is growing out of control. It isn't coming to our feet for training. It isn't coming to our institutions. Its people don't have time for that. And our institutions are not interested in reaching out to such people.

A little digression here. I was asked to go back to Brazil ten years after preaching the gospel of TEE at a Sao Paulo conference of sixty-five seminary types. I was the last Anglo executive director of the Association of Latin American Theological Schools, Northern Region. (In Brazil I was asked to speak out of my territory!) At the end of this four-day conference they formed an association for Theological Education by Extension right on the spot. I didn't propose that they do that. They just did it, and I was very pleased to see it happen. Ten years later I was invited to speak again. They said, "Come back to see what we've done." So I went back and in ten years they had developed a hundred specialized textbooks in Portuguese for that burgeoning extension move-ment! And then, twenty years later (this is 1965–1975–1985), I was asked to go down again. For the first couple of days I was quite in the dark as to what was going on. I found out at a luncheon meeting the second day that they had changed the name of the association. They dropped out the word "extension." It was now just an association of theological schools. After twenty years of what the anthropologists call "cultural leveling" most of the people at the meeting didn't really know much about extension. They wouldn't have ever come to an ACCESS meeting.

I was aghast, and so I shifted gears. In the last two days of the conference I preached the gospel of extension from scratch. As it says in the book of Acts, "and some believed." However, although the seminaries are moving away from extension, the church movement is out of control, and the "standard schools" have little relation to it.

Let's go to India. In India (this is a more recent revelation as far as my own knowledge and experience is concerned) there may very well be more people seriously reading the Bible and following Jesus Christ than the number of those who call themselves Christians or who are called Christians by anybody else. I can't prove this. I don't think I would stake my life on that statement, but even if it is wrong, there is an enormous phenomenon which we are not taking into account, and probably could not meaningfully take into account *using the tools we have*, the techniques we still commonly utilize.

Or go to China. Here's the largest movement in human history that has grown as fast as it has. Out of practically nothing in thirty-five years to 50, 60, 80, 100 million people. Again, I don't stake my life on any of those numbers, but no one questions that it is an enormous phenomenon.

Now, we think of these as house churches. We did not even begin to find out about this until 1979. But of course, there are now also thousands of "regular" churches. The Chinese government grossly underestimated the reality when they opened a hundred churches which they thought would satisfy all the whimpering and make the foreign diplomats happy. Those hundred churches were instantly jammed. "Well," they said, "we'll open another hundred." Pretty soon they had a thousand, and then five thousand, and you know, there is standing room only in these churches. These are the straight churches.

But I'm mainly talking about the fifty thousand *other* churches. What are they really like? I don't think we would want to know in some cases. We would be awed and aghast. They are in the category of the Africa-initiated churches, 50 million in Africa quite possibly, at least an equal number in China; and perhaps half that number of unofficial followers of Christ in India.

It bears mention that the saving grace of the Chinese church is that in most of the house churches the "theological anchor man" is a woman, trained indirectly by women missionaries. The irony is that the male missionaries were expected to carry the load of conveying the biblical inheritance. They were expected, naturally, to teach in proper schools. They did. But note, for every man taught by a man in a "proper" school, dozens of women really learned and loved the Bible by "extension." They were taught with methods which allowed them to learn, despite all their responsibilities, from missionary women who were able to teach the Bible despite all their other responsibilities. What a providence. This extension phenomenon is the principal reason there is a husky church in China with the degree of biblical knowledge it does in fact possess. Korea is similar. The vast majority of the 50,000 house churches under the umbrella of the Full Gospel Church on Yoido Island are essentially pastored and taught by women who have learned the Bible by non-formal methods.

Now, let me warn you: twenty-five years ago, when they figured there were six thousand different denominations in Africa of these strange people—one-third of all these denominations had a *divine person* in their membership and they were called *messianic* for that reason. That's a strange use of the word, but nevertheless, there clearly is wild heresy in many of these churches. And guess what? The cutting edge of Christianity for the last two thousand years has been heresy from the beginning to the end. I mean, there is no version of fast growing Christianity out beyond the bounds of the settled ranks that isn't very obviously in many ways heretical.

But I remember McGavran used to say, "Look, it doesn't matter what these people believe." All the missionaries in the class are shocked and practically fainting away. He would say, "Look. The main thing is, are they reading the Bible? If they keep on reading the Bible, they'll turn out okay." To clinch the logic of that statement, he goes on to say, "For example, the Jehovah's Witnesses read the Bible. You can bet on them. In the long run they will find their way into the traditional churches. The Mormons don't read the Bible; there is no hope for them." Now, that brief comment of McGavran's shouldn't be taken as complete wisdom on those two movements. But in any event, it doesn't really matter; according to McGavran, what they believe will balance out if they are pursuing the living God in the pages of His Word. And it is up to us to get that Word into their hands.

In India illiteracy isn't the same problem. You've got a lot of very highly literate, highly educated, very wealthy people in India who can buy anything that's in the bookstore. In Africa, it is quite different. Many of the leaders of this 50-million block aren't literate. You say, "No wonder they have a lot of heresy." Well, that's not the only reason they are heretical. They know a lot about the Bible. One of the larger of these groups, the Kimbangu movement, for example, was started by Simon Kimbangu.

The Belgians put him in jail. This was Belgian Congo back then. For thirty-eight years he sweltered in prison. And he actually died one year before independence came. Some of the jailers said, "What a shame that the old man didn't get out!" He was such a tremendous influence in the jail. A lot of the prisoners fell under his sway, and the jailers were friendly to him and they said, "Oh, if he had just lived to see this day of independence, he might have been able to rebuild his movement."

No problem. Within a year there were over a million followers. There had only been a hundred thousand when he went to prison. Shortly after that, it was 2 or 3 million and they were all over the middle of Africa. They tried to join the World Council of Churches, but they didn't know about the Lord's Supper so they couldn't become members. So they went back to the Bible, read about it, and said, "Sure, why not?" So now they are members of the World Council of Churches. It isn't that these people are heretical due to rebelling against God. It is because—here's the key word—*access* was not there.

So we've now covered a very large proportion of the Earth's surface. Let's return to the United States. Here I quote Wagner: "Most of the last 25,000 new churches in this country are devoid of seminary-trained leaders. Maybe five percent have seminary-trained leaders." Now, Wagner is not saying this is a good thing at all. He's just describing what is true. But, when you come to the United States there is a different dynamic to some extent. It is not that the people don't have the money to go to school, or that they don't live near enough to go to school, or that they can't leave their families or jobs to go to school. In this country those problems are much more rarely the case.

But even so, in this country the rapidly-growing edge of the Christian movement is with what could be called "non-professional leaders." The same thing is true in England, with five thousand new churches over there. There's practically no connection between these new churches and the standard, traditional, orthodox theological training which we all rightly value so highly. And the reason is practical lack of access. Even in this country.

I remember in Costa Rica, the year I was there studying Spanish, way back in '57, there was a man there who was a CPA, very bright, earnest, a lay believer. He wanted to go to seminary. He lived right *next door* to the seminary, one of the best in Latin America. I said, "You don't have any problem." He said, "Well, you know, I have to work during the day, and they only teach during the day." So he couldn't go to seminary. Now, there was a case of a potential leader being sidetracked.

We are not training the right people, not just because the right people don't want to study, but many times we're not making what we have *accessible* to the right people.

My own personal pilgrimage, you might call it, has put me into contact with a lot of evidence for this. When I first got to Guatemala, I had no idea of what I'm talking about tonight. A friend of mine from seminary days had been there for five years, Jim Emery. He's here tonight. He had already figured out that the key leaders the church really depended upon weren't able to go off to the capital for years to seminary and then come back to their families and their jobs. They couldn't do it. And I have calculated that if you wanted to finance all those real local leaders around the world with proper theological seminary training, it would run about $15 billion per year.

You say, "There must be a lot of these people." That's right. There are about 2 million functional pastors who can't formally qualify for ordination, or who are barely ordained, or who are mostly not ordained simply because they cannot practically penetrate the formal mechanism of theological education even if it might be theoretically accessible to them.

In 1983, Billy Graham brought ten thousand to Amsterdam. He thought he was bringing all the itinerant evangelists of the world. Actually, not one out of ten was an itinerant evangelist in the specialized sense. These were all itinerant evangelists in the ordinary pastoral sense. In Guatemala, every single church was in the business of starting new churches. The average number of new congregations being started would be three. I knew of one church down the mountain from us which had twenty-five new churches going at one point.

When Billy Graham brought them all to Amsterdam, he thought the lectures and inspirational talks he offered them was going to be a great blessing to all these ordinary pastors of the Third World And it was. But, I thought to myself, ten thousand of them—that's a teaspoonful. So then in 1986 he brought another group to Amsterdam, a larger number. I was at that second meeting. It was a wonderful meeting. I met a lot of the two hundred fifty from Guatemala alone. I knew many of them myself. Again, Billy thought, "Now I've done my job. I've gotten all these people some good Bible teaching." (The best exposition at Amsterdam in 1986 was given by his own daughter!) I could have said to Billy, "If you really want all such people to come, you have to expand your attendance from ten thousand to two million.

That's how many functional pastors there are who are literally operating as pastors but do not have a scrap of formal, theological education—and never will, the way things are going. *Access* is the problem.

When I was in Guatemala for ten years, Jim and I worked together very closely and developed what was later referred to as "the Presbyterian experiment," which we called Theological Education by Extension. I edited a book by that title of some six hundred pages which you could look at if you can find a copy. I can't even find my own copy. It has been out of print for quite a while. It will tell you a story of that growth all down through the hemisphere. It is a very interesting thing, it is a fascinating thing, because we didn't foresee running into political problems within the church. All these new people coming into the training program, who were being recruited by the new extension program of the seminary, would then go to the Presbyterian meetings. While many were elders, many of these people were also business people, or lawyers, or attorneys. One of the older pastors, trained as a young person in the former seminary, told me—I'll never forget, sitting in a restaurant one night in the capital city—*"Los misioneros están tratando de destronizar a los pastores,"* "Those missionaries are trying to dethrone the pastors." He ended up running a bookstore. There were people in his church who were more gifted than he was.

He'd gotten into seminary as a young person needing something to eat, wanting something to learn, and he became a pastor, a faithful person, but he was better at running a bookstore than a church. The man who took his place came right out of lay work as an adult and was trained in the seminary by an extension method. It wasn't very long before the number of people that had theological education made accessible to them by extension were able to outvote all the existing pastors. But if that political fact had not been true, our experiment would have been voted out of business. You can be sure of that—a deadly reaction which has erased progress in this area all over the world.

There is a great deal of resistance to change along these lines. Not just resistance from existing pastors who did it in traditional fashion. I was thinking the other day, "How in the world are professors going to effectively use the internet when they never studied by the internet in the first place?" We must pull ourselves up by our bootstraps in such areas because we don't have any experience. Most of our seminaries don't have any professors who got their theological degree in an extension mode. Count on your fingers; I don't think you need any fingers at all. How easily can we see this?

In fact, when I was teaching at Fuller, one of the students in Seattle (which was one of Fuller's extension sites) took all the right courses and inadvertently qualified for an M.A. in Theology. I often went up to Seattle to teach there myself. Nobody but a *kosher* Fuller professor was sent to teach. All the same textbooks, everything. You couldn't possibly say that it was a deficient process. But when a person up there, inadvertently to the school's expectations, took all the courses she needed and then asked for the appropriate degree, there was great consternation back home.

I was in the faculty senate at the time, just eight people: two from each of the three schools, the registrar, and the president. The registrar said, "This is ridiculous. We can't give degrees to people who studied someplace else." I remember the great New Testament expositor, George Eldon Ladd (he was one of the two representatives from the school of theology), I remember him pounding the table and saying, "No one will ever get a degree from Fuller who doesn't come and study here in Pasadena on this campus!" He would exclude even the people who would come right to the campus in the evening to study, *because they were not the proper kind of people.* They were older people, they were more intelligent, they were more stable Christians. I mean, you can't expect *those* people to be ministers! You don't want *them* to get a degree, do you? You've got to keep them out of ordination. That's conventional wisdom.

Now, by the way, thirty years later, you can get an M. Div. degree from Fuller without ever leaving Seattle. But why have we been so slow to come to this?

I remember (not to put Fuller down) I was at Gordon-Conwell one time. This was before the founding of the Ockenga Institute which Bob Freeman ran. For years, I had been in touch with Harold Ockenga, and while I wasn't one of his closest friends, he was one of the most respected people in my life. Many times over a span of thirty years, from the time I was a teenager even, I would send him a letter along with a self-addressed postcard and he would give me an answer to a tough question. I really appreciated that. So we sat in the refectory—the good old Catholic name for the cafeteria—and as we sat across the table he said, "Ralph, tell me what you mean by extension theological education. What would it look like if we were to go that route?"

You can imagine the exhilaration that flowed through my veins at that point. I said, "Well, look. Over the years, Gordon-Conwell has pumped hundreds of wonderful, Evangelical pastors into the veins of the Presbyterian USA denomination." I don't know what the percentage of the students at Gordon-Conwell is now. In those days about two-thirds were going into that one denomination. I said, "Over a period of time you are going to have an influence on the whole denomination, hopefully. But notice how slowly that is going. Suppose you put out 100 new ministers into a body of 18,000 each year. After ten years you've replaced only 1,000 of the 18,000.

"But," I said, "look at it from my experience back in Guatemala. The real leaders, the gifted people that God could readily utilize in a pastoral capacity, are right there in those churches. You go to the 12,000 congregations, you'll find at least an average of three people in each of those congregations who, with the proper theological training, could be ordained and could do a better job than the person who is in the pulpit." And I said, "Stop and think: within four or five years, you could flood the denomination with your people. There would be no way to stop this influence. You could enroll, in one year, 10,000 students to start with." Well, good old Ockenga, brilliant, competent, faithful servant that he was, he could not digest that. But you know, he was really old. He was probably seventy-three years old! (Which is my age right now.)

A similar event took place at my brother's home here in Pasadena. He was very close to David Hubbard and to some of the others in the development dimension at Fuller. My brother invited David Hubbard and me and four or five others down to the house one evening shortly after I came to Fuller from Guatemala. And (this is years earlier than my conversation with Ockenga) David Hubbard asked the same question: "After all this talk about principles and theory and distant places, what would Fuller actually look like if we were to go that route?" Probably I wasn't as cautious and careful and thoughtful and wise as I tried to be when I talked later to Ockenga. I said, "Well, Dave, it wouldn't be any problem to explain this. First of all you would shut the campus down and you would establish maybe twenty-eight extension centers in Southern California, and enroll probably 4,000 people," and so on. I couldn't even get into the second paragraph. What I said was perfectly possible. It was perfectly uninteresting. Fuller was intent on being conventional. What was good for church leadership had become a question of what was good for the establishment of a conventional school.

Well, they did make some moves when Robert Munger came on the faculty two or three years later. He also had similar interests. He was very much a man of the church, and he was very eager for the seminary to make a contribution to the church. He, probably more than any other person, helped Fuller into an extension mode. But after ten years in that mode they still would not give a degree to somebody who studied in Seattle. There was no reason they couldn't, except, well—this is a pervasive problem in human society—when the means to an end becomes the end, you are in big trouble.

Remember, all of us here represent "means:" schools, schools that are set up to provide a certain service. Princeton Seminary's catalog says, "We exist to serve the church." I think that's an honest statement, but it is not accurate. Princeton Seminary has other goals that it has to deal with. Intermediate goals, sure, but *intermediate goals are the worst enemy of the real goals if you can't see beyond those intermediate goals.* They have the intermediate goal of paying all those professors. That means they have the intermediate goal of getting enough money in, not only in tuition but in donations. They have a lot of things to do to keep alive and to keep going and to keep their building program in mind and their Speer Library and all that vital stuff. *They've got enough to think about without thinking about the church.* Now, they probably do think about the church, but this recent book entitled *Being There* highlights one of the mainstream seminaries, and gives you one of the most dismal views you can imagine. I just blanch at the thought. I can't imagine *Christian Century* even publishing this review (of *Being There*) of what actually goes on in schools for whom apparently *the means has become the end.* The real end is out of sight.

Years ago, long after I got to Guatemala, Jim and I had worked on our TEE program and we sold the idea to other missions in Guatemala, then to other countries. Then, an association of theological schools was formed in the northern region, which means seventeen out of twenty-one Latin American countries were in this association called ALET. I was the second executive director of that association. Our perspectives about extension were woven right into the structure of that association (not like the ATS). That took me all over the place, to different countries.

In those days there was very little resistance in the mission field to ideas that would nourish the church. I think missionaries, most of whom do not spend their full time in schools, are very much more alive to the possibilities of theological extension. That's why our ACCESS conference theme this year, "Global Access," is so important. We are talking about the global reality. Now that may shake us up just a little, because all these reviews, all these books are slavishly confined to the USA. In any case, going around to these different countries, visiting these different schools, a great deal boomed into action. And then eventually we were going around the world under the sponsorship of the EFMA. Wagner went around the world with Ralph Covell. Covell and I went around the world the next year sowing the seeds of TEE. And then Wayne Weld, later a professor at North Park Seminary in Chicago, did his doctoral dissertation at Fuller on the development of the movement, and produced a hefty book entitled *The World Directory of TEE.* At the time his book was produced, 100,000 people were studying for the ministry under what might have been 400 to 500 schools around the world.

But then, while that early TEE movement to some extent is still there, I have often referred to it as collapsing. I am not sure what our ACCESS society will do about that collapse but I am sure of what it can do. *The major impediment which withdrew those schools from helping people into the ministry by extension was the fact that this pattern was not being followed in the United States.* Why? To a great extent what's done in this country tyrannizes what can or can't be done in the mission field either near or far.

Now, the other mission field I talked about, these burgeoning churches, they don't even know how you spell "seminary." They are not influenced by what seminaries will or won't do in this country. But in any event, gradually the residential schools of the non-Western world—about 4,000 now—realized they weren't doing what was conventional in the USA, and gave up TEE in order to be "proper."

So when Bob Freeman told me, "You know, we had to accept this second best—we couldn't get to the field," I said, "Listen, what you are doing is more important than what any missionary in the world is doing, because you are helping a prestigious seminary to establish a pattern which will then buttress what ought to continue to happen overseas."

And then, of course, the "degree-completion" movement came into being. Again, it is not a movement that was the result of people getting down on their knees and praying, "Now, Lord, are we really serving the church?" It was a movement that was pressured financially. In order to survive, schools were going off campus to teach. Many were so scared to death they were going to go broke that the accrediting associations didn't say anything when they did finally begin to teach away from the campus.

Now I understand from Dr. Oosting that the accrediting associations are beginning to take a bead and to shoot at these degree completion programs to make sure they increase the quality and time and all that up to the norm, and so forth. But, see, it is very, very crucial what the pattern is in this country as you look back across the world. In fact, we fight not against flesh and blood. We fight against mammoth cultural forces: the degree-mania of our time, especially in Asia, the inflation of units, the redefinition of all kinds of things. *But the worst is what I would call institutionalization, which replaces the end with the means.* Institutions of any kind begin to decline when they become first concerned about their own existence.

I think, for example, of the welfare workers in Wisconsin. I read an article in the *Los Angeles Times* which said that Wisconsin is making remarkable progress in getting people into jobs and getting them off welfare. The welfare workers can only stay in business if there are lots of people on welfare. Their biggest problem is not the people on welfare, but the people in the welfare offices who are more interested in keeping their jobs than they are in getting people off welfare. Now, translate that into the seminaries. The biggest problem with the seminaries is that they don't want what is needed most. The seminaries think they can stay in business only if they have residential students. And staying in business comes first.

There are other ways that people can measure progress. The post office, for instance. There is some link between how much mail comes in and what the people get paid. I know that to be true, because they are so eager to get the business away from the other post office down the street! That could only be true if there is something in it for them. All kinds of institutions measure themselves by different things. But when an institution comes to the point when its leaders measure themselves by how many students there are or what their enrollment is—that's only a means to the end. The real question is, who's there? Or more precisely, *who is it that isn't there?*

I knew John Wimber, a local boy here in Southern California, before he was famous. He never went to seminary to study. He went to seminary to teach. And his Vineyard movement has 200, 300, 500 churches, I don't know. Those people don't go to seminary. They should. I'm the first one to say that what seminary has to offer would be very significant to his people, but somehow the access isn't there. On and on.

We could say the same for many, many leaders in America today. *The growing edge of the American church has had to learn to do without the seminaries.* Not because the seminaries don't have something crucial to offer. Not even because they don't know how to offer it. It is because they have not decided to offer it.

I'll give you a case in point. Not long ago, the seminaries balked and screamed at the thought of offering a two-year degree. True or false? It is true. That was a tremendous, traumatic thing for them to offer a two-year degree, because they didn't want it to cut into their three-year degree. I remember sitting at dinner in the home of a professor at Westminster Seminary. (I'd better not mention any names.) I was praising him for their downtown M.A. program in missiology in the heart of Philadelphia. I no sooner got halfway into the sentence when he said, "Yeah, but you can't get an M.Div. on the basis of that program. You have to start all over. You have to come back to this campus and start from scratch if you are going to get an M.Div." He was protecting a certain program. I don't think his main concern was what happened to those poor folks down in Philadelphia. He was primarily *thinking about the means rather than the end.* And on and on. You could find hundreds of examples of this.

So I just leave you with this to think about. There are probably a number of positive things we could do differently that would enable some insight to come from this topic. But I feel I will have done something even if all I do is identify the problem: we are teaching the wrong people rather than the right people.

During the Second World War, the Navy paid for the University of Wisconsin to prepare all of their college courses for extension use. The University of Wisconsin is a very high-level, high-class, respectable school, but they didn't have any trouble doing that. Just like that, an entire college curriculum was now available to anyone in the Navy, anywhere.

But they drove a hard bargain. "When the war's over, every single book you still have in your hands will be burned, because we want to go back to our cloistered, hallowed school system. We don't want to continue to benefit, like we did, two and a half million students." How do you like that? Simply because they were paid to do it, they could do it. There's nothing mysterious about extension technique.

It is pretty obvious how to help people that are out there. You don't have to be a brain! It is the question of whether we *want* to do it, not whether we are *able* to do it. *What we do in this country has overwhelming impact upon schools around the world.* Right now most of the schools around the world are following us and going in the wrong direction!

Question Period

Question: How do you evaluate the view of some denominations about the professionalization of the pastorate as a requirement, for instance with an M.Div? What kind of effect does that have?

Winter: It is like shooting yourself in the foot. Really. That's the historical fact. Every single denomination in this country that requires formal, extensive, graduate, professional training for ordination is now going downhill. There are no exceptions in the whole world. In fact people have gotten the wrong impression about seminaries, joking about cemeteries, and so on. They assume that whoever the students are, that with a good curriculum and a pastorally-experienced faculty, the students will graduate as good pastors. Rather, even a poor curriculum with poor faculty would graduate good pastors *if highly gifted, mature Christians were the students!* Seminaries have no policy of turning such people away. They simply don't make sure to give access to them—which is something that ought to be their highest priority.

Question: You have identified the problem. What's your prognosis for the future? Are you optimistic or pessimistic?

Winter: In this country it is a little different from what it would be in the rest of the world. I've already described the fact that most of the growing Christianity of the world does not even know what a seminary is, so in a certain sense, don't worry about Christianity. It is going to take care of itself. This is the outrageous phenomenon—most people think that we've got to send more missionaries and more money just to keep Christianity from collapsing! It is almost the other way around! We could double our missionary force, and we would only slow down those church movements that would buy into our method of preventing real leaders from ordination. I'm very optimistic about the church if we can stop preventing its real leaders from leading. However, I don't think there's much hope for these 4,000 schools in the so-called mission lands unless they can truly help the churches.

Question: Do you want to comment on the curricula being designed around the Great Commission as well as the Great Commitment?

Winter: Since the average evangelical seminary is mainly talking about the Old Testament or the New Testament or church history at any given time—remember, that's their three-fold core emphasis—it is not very hard for that material to be interpreted in terms of global mission. This is what we've done in our 320 lessons that run all the way through seminary content. For example, we've been overjoyed to discover thirty-six missiological issues right in the book of Genesis. Normally, people study Genesis in one school and missiology in another school, and when they study Genesis, they don't study the missiological issues of that narrative. When they study missiology, they don't study Genesis. The two things are separated out. But the missiological issues in the book of Genesis can well be integrated into standard curricula. I don't think it is very *difficult*.

But, on the other hand, it is very *unlikely* to be integrated in most schools for the simple reason that those who handle the Bible don't normally think in terms of global mission.

I would just say, that in terms of optimism or pessimism, it is sort of like the New Testament situation where the Jews could be pessimistic about the expansion of their faith by not recognizing that the Greeks were of the same faith. So they were pessimistic when they could have been optimistic. Later on, the Catholics were very pessimistic when they saw the breakaway of what was later called Protestantism. They were pessimistic when they should have been optimistic. We are in a similar situation today. We can cross the world, and say, "What's going on?" And some people are very pessimistic about the heresies and the abounding diversities and the confusion of the global Christian movement when maybe they should be very optimistic. So it is partly a question of what you are looking at, and from what perspective.

Question: Would you like to comment on the point that overseas the theological vacuum is being filled particularly by the Bible college movement and extensions of that movement?

Winter: I wish it were true. It is true that there are 4,000 schools. We have a book produced by the World Evangelical Fellowship's Theological Commission, listing 4,000 schools, at least 3,000 of these being in the non-Western world. And these schools have students, many young people. But, and here is the crucial point, many of them are more concerned about keeping their enrollment up instead of finding and educating—by whatever means necessary—the actual, real, mature, gifted leaders in their associated church movements. It is not a question of whether we think of humble Bible schools or well-endowed seminaries. The key question is whether or not they are offering access to the real leaders of their movement.

However, even if they had nothing but proven, gifted leaders in their schools (which is highly unlikely if they are running daytime classes), their entire number of students would still be only a drop in the bucket compared to the massive number of functional pastors running the churches, who can't make it to school because they are busy planting new churches, holding down bi-vocational jobs and raising families as well.

Thus, I'm saying that the theological education one receives is not just valid and useful only if it is just like what we do in this country. What we do in this country just won't fit in most situations overseas. Note that I have no problem at all with the so-called "scurrilous" Bible schools.

In fact, I feel a little bit funny that this association, after twenty years, has sort of accidentally demoted a lot of schools because they didn't fit a particular monocultural pattern. We say you can't be an institutional member of this association unless you do certain things a certain way, which for the most part has very little relevance to the real world, much less the non-Western world. In that momentary—and I would think erroneous—conclusion our association did, I feel, wound itself in terms of recognizing the validity of Bible training of many other sorts.

But even if you take all of that into account, the ordaining force in most mission-related churches (which is a very substantial part of what we would call recognizable Christianity around the world), rules out people for ordination if they have scurrilous training. (I use the word *scurrilous* playfully—I refer to what some people *consider* scurrilous.) There's always going to be one person who went off overseas to Columbia Bible College, and came back with a "proper" degree. From then on, all other education is no longer considered worthy and is demoted to secondary status.

The Student Volunteer Movement sent people into Africa. Kefa Sempangi in his book, *A Distant Grief,* observed how new missionaries who came out with college degrees (they were the first large numbers of missionaries with college degrees) discovered African pastors—can you believe it?—pastors, ordained ministers, who didn't have a college degree! And they pushed them out of their pulpits. It took forty years for the student volunteers to recover a missiology that would understand the need for shifting gears.

Probably the most remarkable use of Bible schools that I know of would be in Latin America by the Assemblies of God in their so-called "night Bible schools." These night Bible schools, first of all, were in the evening. That means they were *accessible*. As far as I'm concerned, a night school is an extension operation. Distance, frankly, has nothing to do with it. Remember the CPA who lived next door to the seminary? "Distance" education would have solved his problem, but the distance in his case was not geographical.

In any case, those night Bible schools fueled the church with an amazing amount of biblical knowledge and stature in the Word that enabled its students to be elevated into the ministry over a long process which was very careful in selection and so forth. Thus, in the so-called Pentecostal movement very rarely is a man ordained who is the wrong man. In our movement once "formal" schooling gets a hammerlock on who gets ordained in the church, the church says, "Okay, we won't ordain anybody unless he or she goes to our formal school."

Once they make that fatal step, they've ruled out most of the gifted people who could be leaders in the church. And that's what the Assemblies of God in Latin America *did not do*. And their movement is now so strong you practically have to be a Pentecostal if you are going to go to Latin America. Talk about pessimism and optimism. The mainstream churches that we think of as respectable churches in this country are not only half dead in Latin America, they are almost completely invisible—they are overwhelmingly outnumbered! They're zany rare objects by comparison to the new mainstream of Latin America. The same would be true in slightly different form in most other parts of the world.

Further Comment on the Actual Track Record of Evangelical Educational Structures:

ACCESS is a society of schools which has learned how to educate at a distance. Our experience over the last twenty-six years has proven that real education does not have to take place through classroom incarceration. We in ACCESS hold the key to an educating lifestyle that allows people both to learn and at the same time attend to the meaningful duties and challenges of real life instead of succumbing to the culturally approved years-upon-years spent in an artificial school world that is numbing and perverting.

When, without blinking, we measure education by the number of years in school, when we say someone is more highly educated than someone else just because he has lost more years in the school world, we are confusing *the means* with *the end*.

But all this is merely basic to the specific application of tonight's topic. Several examples may illuminate this background in order for the foreground of the needs of the church to be seen more clearly.

Let's look first at Moody Bible Institute. It started out as an evening continuing education school for the thousands of adults who had been caught up in an immense revival of faith that swept this country and England, in which Moody was a principal force. This vast revival produced the school, not the reverse. For various reasons, the Moody Bible Institute soon transitioned into schooling young people during the day. It did not give up its continuing education component because its extension activities were and are substantial. It is just that the day-school activities are what people now think of when they think of Moody Bible Institute. I think that the transition was not unreasonable at the time. The older students at night wanted their children to be exposed to vital Bible teaching. And the teachers could not make a living just teaching in the evening. Furthermore, as a faculty gathered subjects arose for discussion that may have been tangential. For example, for some years Moody's faculty was known for its mastery of a detailed countdown of eschatology. It is not that Moody has not performed a great service to the church. The fact that 157 Bible institutes jumped into existence confirms the existence of the market which they served. But in many respects this vast Bible institute phenomenon became one huge mistake.

Let's behold something similar: the costly transition of A. B. Simpson's earlier school in New York City to today's Nyack College up the Hudson River. That occurred during a nearly full century in which the 157 similar Bible institutes came into existence and then one by one marched out of existence.

In addition to the shift away from training adult leaders, I am convinced that a major mistake made by this entire spiritually vital tradition took place when they turned attention to young people—for whom the secular world has a prescribed pattern for growing up. This second mistake was the assumption that the cultural norms of the secular culture could be ignored. Instead of adding Bible to what people had already learned or were learning in the public schools (as was and is the case of the evening adult students) the Bible institute movement soon became a generally irretrievable replacement for a number of significant years—three or four—of secular school experience.

It ought not to be a surprise, now 100 years later, that this grand experiment died, an experiment that once flowered and was first replaced by Bible colleges, and then more and more by what are called Christian colleges, which do now finally adhere to the secular norms.

But think of all that happened and did not happen during the hundred years of transition: the tens of thousands, yea hundreds of thousands, perhaps millions, of evangelical youth who were given diplomas that would not admit them to further education or to the professions, Congress, whatever! The evangelical movement has only recently begun to integrate Christian knowledge with secular standards and become a substantial force in the secular sphere of our society.

A similar thing continues to happen in the realm of the seminaries. They too continue to pump out degrees that in the secular world are unintelligible or irrelevant or both. Pity the seminary graduate who would like to think that his three or four years of seminary will be as respected in the secular world as is a Ph.D. from, say, Seattle Pacific University, which is one of only a handful of evangelical schools yet offering a Ph.D.

But this adds an important note. Seattle Pacific, and the holiness tradition in general—add in the Christian church (Churches of Christ tradition, and yes, the Roman Catholic tradition)—did not go headlong into the offbeat pattern, the Bible institute pattern. Seattle Pacific, Abilene, Pepperdine offered Ph.D. degrees long before the Calvinistic Bible Institute pattern yielded to that. Moody, for example, was one of the first institutes to exist but one of the last to offer a regionally accredited B.A. degree. How long before Moody offers a Ph.D.? The irony is that Wheaton College avoided the institute detour partly because of its early holiness influence, but does not to this day offer a Ph.D. program.

Marvelously, and recently, some major evangelical seminaries have begun to move toward the university pattern and offer a Ph.D., although most of them are still loath to give up their questionable M.Div. detour.

Now, all of this is an historical perspective on the shifting pressures of society and of the needs of society in regard to the structure and program of the schools. We do well not to underestimate the power of cultural traditions. If it took the entire Calvinistic evangelical tradition a hundred years to make up its mind about the wrapping paper of its educational product, what will it take to analyze afresh the essential problems which it came into existence to address?

The reason ACCESS is so potentially cogent is that although daytime schooling may be appropriate as a child-care mechanism for small children, or even for slightly older children, the same kind of incarceration for young people and adults replaces the possibility of significant participation in the real world. Years ago I defined extension education for myself very simply as "that form of education which does not disrupt the student's productive relation to society." Whether by night classes, weekend classes, vacation classes, part-time classes, internet activities, or whatever, if it is possible for a student to get on with life, to gradually support his existence by giving back to society something for his own support, then the ACCESS ideal has been achieved—as a procedural goal, at least.

THOUGHTS ABOUT JIM EMERY (AND TEE) ON THE OCCASION OF HIS FUNERAL AUGUST 27, 1999
by RALPH D. WINTER

I first met Jim in 1946 when we both attended Princeton Theological Seminary. Before that I had heard a little about the very serious church he had come from in Schenectady, NY, where a whole stream of General Electric engineers had been highjacked into the ministry by the legendary pastor, Herbert McKeel.

We had a lot in common. Both with engineering training. Both setting out now to do other kinds of engineering. Both just out of the U.S. Navy. Both creatively skeptical about the way things are, and enthusiastic about not leaving them that way. That one academic year ('46-'47) also took us both to Toronto to the first of the famous series of so-called Urbana student missionary conferences. It brought us both into contact with Christy Wilson Jr., who founded that series of conferences and who even earlier worked with us to organize a student mission retreat for Princeton Seminary students. For speakers we got both Eugene Nida of the American Bible Society (one of the two student geniuses—Nida and Kenneth Pike—who helped found the Wycliffe Bible Translators), and Bruce Metzger, a Princeton Seminary faculty member whom we greatly admired and whom we wished to get more interested in missions!

That crammed year, 1946-47, was all I spent at Princeton at that time. I did not return to finish until 1953. When I finally graduated in 1956 and was headed for Guatemala, I had no idea that Jim and Gennet would have landed there years before. It was a very pleasant surprise. By now Jim was a veteran from whom I had a great deal to learn.

Gennet has asked me to speak of Jim and TEE. For me this all began when I first got to Guatemala. I was stunned to hear Jim say that dozens of little coastal churches (which it was his assignment to assist) were starved for ordained leadership for the simple reason that the real leaders could not possibly pull away from family and jobs to go off to the Presbyterian seminary 150 miles away in the capital city. He had persuaded the powers-that-be that the seminary needed to be moved out to where most of the churches were—in the rural areas.

This major decision had plunged him into literally buying land and building a new seminary campus in a tiny sleepy coastal town called San Felipe.

Although I worked in the highlands I became a member of the new board of directors. An additional barrier remained. It was still true that the real leaders of the rural congregations could not spend a lot of time on the grounds of the seminary even though it was now much closer than 150 miles. The next major step was to decentralize the instruction, to use the new campus as a *source* of outreach rather than as a *destination* for younger boarding students to come and live. This was quite a wrench. I was on the seminary board, Jim was on the faculty. It was an event directly involving only a few people.

But reverberations from capital city pastors became even more intense. At a crucial synod meeting this new, even more radical decentralization of the seminary arose as an explosive issue. The first move to a rural location had pulled the board out of the hands of city people. This second move all but junked the on-campus student pattern and allowed the seminary program for the first time to enroll older men—in most cases people who had already been elected elders in their local churches. Oops, the familiar young, male students were no longer as visible.

Thus, at a key meeting a city pastor stood up and complained that seminary students were now mainly just laymen, not young men on their way to ministerial ordination—in the more familiar pattern. The atmosphere was tense.

I'll never forget that moment Jim stood up and addressed the 200 or so pastors and elders at this annual synod meeting. He was the only missionary who when he stood up to say something was seriously listened to with respect by both nationals and missionaries. He picked up on the objection that the seminary student body—now scattered all over and not living right at the seminary—was no longer a dozen or so young men who needed a place to sleep and something to eat, but was now about sixty-five in number and mainly older leaders who were being at that moment castigated for being mere laymen. He said simply, "Look, what is so unusual about laymen in seminary? I was a layman when I was in seminary; so were you; all of us went to seminary as laymen."

Between the lines of the pastor's objection was the disturbing fact, of course, that the new seminary student was now a more mature, impressive leader. Some were doctors and lawyers in the city. Young city pastors worried that they might lose their pulpits. (Some did.) Word had gone around that *"los misioneros están tratando de destronizar a los pastores."* (Those missionaries are trying to dethrone the pastors.) True, the seminary in this new system was looking for and finding those people Jim had talked to me about earlier—the real leaders who were already to be found in the local congregations. The seminary, through its new extension system, was now being reengineered to be able to offer them the necessary qualifications for ordination.

This embryonic life would have been aborted, this major threat to the status quo would, in fact, have been voted out of existence had it not been true that the rural vote now consisted mainly of elders who were actually enrolled in this new seminary extension program!

Thus, hanging on by its fingernails, this major mutation in how the church gets its leadership survived. It incorporated the novel idea that pastoral education was not a matter of how many years you had soaked in school but who you were and the functional nature of what you learned. The rural Presbyteries had long ordained people with fewer school years behind them than the city pastors. Now the seminary had three distinct levels of pastoral education, all of them equivalent for the purposes of ordination. All of a sudden the seminary was no longer a detour to a distant place accessible only to untried younger men. Now the church could harvest for its leadership its real leaders, and all of this was the upshot of Jim's insight. I was glad to help make it happen.

The ideas spread. My wife and I then went on to help set up a pre-seminary extension program which enabled rural people whose schooling only went through the third grade to attain the coveted sixth-grade diploma—which was the minimum required by the seminary. Six major missions in Guatemala were involved in this program of more than 1,000 students—and the seminary goal gained visibility, too. Soon, down through the hemisphere and then globally, "the Guatemala Presbyterian Plan" was seriously considered. I was involved in much of this and though I constantly referred to Jim's basic contribution, my name became associated with the movement more than his. Though I was in the limelight, I edited a 700 page book chronicling these developments and Jim's chapter is the very first one. Others took up the cause. Peter Wagner, Covell, Mulholland, later Kinsler and Weld. All of these aided in the movement, but the basic insight was Jim's.

At one point the movement involved over 100,000 leaders training for ministry. But the basic insight gradually faded. The mechanics of teaching began to loom large in discussions, the threat to existing residential schools raised its head, and existing pastors who had gone through residential schooling felt threatened. To school directors, the negative example of the U.S. carried great weight even though the really growing movements both at home and abroad bypass the standard selection pattern. Not enough people today realize what Jim was saying: he was not proposing a new kind of education as much as he was seeking to educate the right people. His presence is needed more now than ever.

While Jim was bold and determined and very self-assured about his personal conclusions, he was not an aggressive extrovert. I never witnessed him in anything like a shouting match. While of a retiring, respectful manner, he was not hesitant or reticent about his own opinions and, to my knowledge, was never truly overawed by anyone, although he held great respect for some little-recognized people like Georges Barrois, a former Dominican priest who was a professor at Princeton Seminary when we were there. He was, appropriately, unimpressed by the "culture" of which others could be very proud.

Jim therefore could easily be underestimated. He was in some ways shy. His high wall of defense of his privacy was his ready jest. Talking to the real Jim was not a privilege he extended to everyone.

On the other hand I can't imagine him ever trying to belittle anyone or put anyone down.

My own admiration for him is boundless. I don't believe I have ever had a better friend.

Did he have to die so soon? Seems like cancer is pulling down all kinds of key people ahead of their time. Apparently about half of all Americans will contract some form of cancer before they die. I have done a crash course in cancer in the last three years of my wife's slow-growing bone cancer. Americans now spend less than half of one percent of their cancer money on research into the nature of the disease. All the rest goes for treatment after cancer has struck. Only a handful of people on the planet are trying to understand the nature of cancer. Isn't that kind of shortsighted?

But of course we have no theology of fighting disease—our classical theologians didn't know germs existed. Most people still don't. Our ancient theologians, like Augustine, added a pagan assumption into the Christianity of the Bible: not Satan but God is the author of disease—therefore we can't fight it! Too late for Jim.